Architecture of Skidmore, Owings & Merrill, 1973–1983

Architecture of Skidmore, Owings & Merrill, 1973–1983

Introduction and Regional Prefaces by Albert Bush-Brown

The Monacelli Press

Copyright © 1983, 2009 by Skidmore, Owings & Merrill LLP

All rights reserved. Published in the United States by The Monacelli Press,
a division of Random House, Inc., New York

This work was originally published in different form in a bilingual edition in Germany by Verlag Gerd
Hatje, Stuttgart, and in the United States by Van Nostrand Reinhold Company, New York, in 1983.

The Monacelli Press is a trademark of Random House, Inc.

Library of Congress Cataloging-in-Publication Data
Skidmore, Owings & Merrill.
SOM : architecture of Skidmore, Owings & Merrill, 1973–1983 / introduction and regional prefaces
by Albert Bush-Brown. — 1st ed.
p. cm.
Originally published: Skidmore, Owings & Merrill architecture and urbanism, 1973–1983. Bilingual
ed. Stuttgart, Germany : Verlag Gerd Hatje, 1983 and New York : Van Nostrand Reinhold Co., 1983.
ISBN 978-1-58093-222-6
1. Skidmore, Owings & Merrill. 2. Architecture—United States—History—20th century. I. Title. II.
Title: Skidmore, Owings & Merrill architecture and urbanism, 1973–1983.
NA737.S53A4 2009c
720.92'2—dc22   2009009235

Printed in China

www.monacellipress.com

10 9 8 7 6 5 4 3 2 1
First edition

Project Editors: Elizabeth Harrison Kubany and Landis Livingston Carey

Jacket design: Pentagram Design Inc.
With acknowledgment to Chermayeff & Geismar

Contents

Skidmore, Owings & Merrill

Partners 1973–1983

Nathaniel A. Owings
Gordon Bunshaft
J. Walter Severinghaus
William E. Hartmann
Walter A. Netsch
John O. Merrill, Jr.
Roy O. Allen
Edward C. Bassett
Bruce J. Graham
David A. Pugh
Myron Goldsmith
Albert Lockett
Walter H. Costa
Donald C. Smith
Marc E. Goldstein
Fazlur R. Khan
Whitson M. Overcash
James R. DeStefano
Robert Diamant
Thomas J. Eyerman
Richard E. Lenke
Michael A. McCarthy
Leon Moed
John K. Turley
Gordon Wildermuth
David M. Childs
Srinivasa Iyengar
Walter W. Arensberg
Richard H. Ciceri
Lawrence S. Doane
Parambir S. Gujral
Raul de Armas
William M. Drake
Richard C. Keating
John H. Winkler
James W. Christensen
Peter Hopkinson
Robert A. Hutchins
Roger M. Seitz
Adrian D. Smith
Kenneth A. Soldan
Robert P. Holmes
Maris Peika
Robert Armsby
Richard C. Foster
Richard A. Giegengack
Diane Legge Lohan

Introduction

"SOM 1973–1983" reveals the architectural response of Skidmore, Owings & Merrill to a decade that greatly changed American society. Whereas its two earlier histories had recorded SOM's dramatic designs for a broad array of public and private clients, this book reveals a marked narrowing in America's sponsorship. Both federal and state governments slowed their construction programs, and, except for the ascendant pharmaceutical, energy and electronics industries, few manufacturing corporations commissioned new buildings. Like the industrial corporation, the university was no longer expanding, and although a few notable museums added large wings, America's enormous postwar expansion of its cultural institutions came to a pause. The decade 1973–83 belonged to the urban office tower. Supplying rental office space, many towers were built by developers who, managing investments made by foreign and American speculators, set architectural constraints SOM had seldom known in earlier work for corporate patrons.

With its industrial and institutional structure in place, America in 1973 still needed to renew its worn cities, but, continuing a half-century surge, the suburbs rather than inner cities attracted investment, and urban renewal was deflected by political and economic events: Watergate ended Nixon's presidency and any chance for its urban program; withdrawal from the Vietnam War raised hopes for urban investment, but the 1973 Arab oil embargo caused an energy shortage, followed by increased oil prices, general inflation, twenty percent interest rates, and reduced urban investment. Before the pace of urban reform slackened, SOM completed important urban designs for Sacramento, Chicago and San Antonio, but, by 1975, impoverished Detroit and Cleveland, like other Northern industrial cities, could not finance their own renewal, and New York City barely avoided default on its borrowings.

Frustrated by a barren domestic economy, America's technical and organizational talent sought work abroad. Some of Canada's great developers called SOM to Calgary and Edmonton. In 1974, SOM was invited to send architects and planners to Algeria, Egypt and Iran, and, in 1975, Saudi Arabia asked SOM to design Jeddah's International Airport and Haj Terminal. The Algerian and Saudi Arabian projects helped carry SOM through the bleak years 1975–77 when oil shifted the locus of economic power and the American economy sagged.

When, after 1976, foreign and American developers began to invest in office construction in American cities, SOM designed distinctive towers that lofted rich and often splendid forms into America's skylines. Thus, the year 1983 brought SOM to an architectural pinnacle: San Francisco's Crocker Center and Federal Reserve Bank, Los Angeles' Crocker Center [1], Houston's Allied Bank, Chicago's One Magnificent Mile [2], Atlanta's Georgia-Pacific, Miami's Southeast Financial Center, and New York City's Irving Trust [3] and 780 Third Avenue – all neared completion as 1983 approached.

In comparison with New York's Lever House [4] or Chicago's Inland Steel [5] of the 1950's, SOM's new buildings often resolve complexities imposed by irregular sites, mixed functions, and struggles to supply maximum rentable space at least cost. The resulting forms depart from the earlier technological imagery. For more than two decades, Lever House and Inland Steel had inspired the architectural profession. Elite corporate clients, such as Chase Manhattan Bank and Connecticut General, had set the corporate style by giving their own companies luxurious, prestigious, often art-filled occupancy [6, 7]. Lever House and Inland Steel confined narrow sunlighted slabs to the edges of their sites and offered air space, sidewalk plazas and glazed lobbies. Today, their elegance looks innocent: naive about those expediencies prompted by borrowed dollars and rental occupancies, modest in height and land coverage, indifferent about garages or concessionary services, cavalier about historic context, and almost oblivious to energy conservation. As the 1980's neared, their form came under attack. Its alleged functionalism was disputed; its glazed, mullioned expression and orthogonal order were demeaned; and its isolation and singular occupancy were rejected as an urban planning model. In the ultimate accusation, the technological symbol was maligned for being abstract, metallic and empty.

Clearly, that ultimate criticism springs from changed aesthetic values. SOM partners in the 1970's were less and less wedded to Lever House or Inland Steel. In collaboration with other architectural firms, SOM/San Francisco designed the Bank of America

1 Crocker Center, Los Angeles, California.
2 One Magnificent Mile, Chicago, Illinois.
3 Irving Trust Operations Center, New York, New York.

1

4 Lever House, New York, New York.
5 Inland Steel Building, Chicago, Illinois.
6 Connecticut General Life Insurance Headquarters, Bloomfield, Connecticut.

4

5

6

1

before 1970. By 1980, SOM/Chicago at Chicago's One Magnificent Mile and SOM/San Francisco at Houston's InterFirst Plaza modelled remarkably fresh images. Their form is prismatic and elusive where, before, it was planear and literal; it is attentive to adjoining streets, buildings and vistas, and it relies on faceted mass, rhythms, textures and color, without exaggerating structural systems to gain formal impact. Incorporating public spaces and circulation, the new buildings often combine retail, office and, sometimes, residential space, revealing a change in urban goals as well as aesthetic form.

Still, SOM's buildings of 1973–83 continue SOM's commitment to originate beautiful form from technology and to perfect each building's total performance. Those hallmarks are not easily maintained. With thirty-three partners located in nine regional offices, SOM works hard at an ideal: vibrant design developed by coordinated experts bringing each project from client's stated need to completed building on scheduled date, at projected cost, and to satisfied occupancy. One SOM partner speaks of the "total integrity of completed projects." Another claims that SOM is a "precision instrument." What is steadily impressive is SOM's drive to perfect artistic expression of technology through spatial and sculptural order.

SOM's growth as a partnership began almost 50 years ago. Founded in 1936, SOM started with a commitment to modern design, without traditional antecedents. Looking back, retired partner William Hartmann outlines SOM's development in three stages: 1936 through 1946, when, following the World's Fair projects and buildings for the H.J. Heinz Company [8], SOM designed the Oak Ridge Laboratories during World War II; 1946 through 1973, when SOM advanced the postwar conversion to a civilian economy by meeting needs for hospitals, universities, and office buildings, epitomized by Chicago's John Hancock Building [9] and Sears Tower [10]; and 1973 forward, when SOM built chiefly office towers while awaiting America's long-deferred decision to renew its industries, housing, and transit systems. Now, according to Hartmann, SOM and other American architectural firms are constrained from applying their enormous talents because the American economy has retreated from such investments.

Laments about America's neglect of its great architectural talent rose at a time when SOM's partnership was changing. Starting with an office in Chicago in 1936 and soon thereafter opening in New York, followed by offices in San Francisco and Portland, SOM in the 1970's established fully staffed, partner-led offices in Washington, Houston, Los Angeles, Denver and Boston. By late 1981, the 9 offices had more than 2,100 members. Of 33 General Partners in 1980, 75 percent had entered the firm as young professionals since 1960, 80 percent had become General Partners since 1970, and, of all 33, a promising 55 percent had become General Partners since 1975.

The young partners' ascendancy coincided with the retirement of many partners who had led SOM through the three stages Hartmann outlined. The decade 1973–83 brought the retirement of founding partner Nathaniel Owings; New York's Gordon Bunshaft, Walter Severinghaus and Roy Allen; Chicago's Walter Netsch and Myron Goldsmith; and San Francisco's Edward C. Bassett. Their eminent buildings had created SOM's reputation. Who would succeed Bunshaft in SOM/New York, which had a complete turn-over? Who would continue the deft structural insights lost when Chicago partner Fazlur Khan died of a heart attack in 1982? Unlike law firms, no previous American architectural partnership had survived with distinction into a third or fourth generation. Had SOM's retired leaders nurtured continuity and succession? Viewing SOM's future from his Chicago office General Partner Thomas Eyerman expected SOM's leadership to emerge through "creative dissidence." Willing to test their faith in self-renewal, SOM chose to spawn great artists by placing promising young design partners in charge of new regional offices and large projects. Hope lay in the belief that SOM's partnership would help the young partners grow, as Bassett's special vision had assembled and nurtured artists in SOM's San Francisco office. Still, the young and regionally dispersed partners had inherited modern architecture as sculptural form without knowing it as an agency of social reform, the most eloquent image for organizing society since the Renaissance. In that gap lay the great risk that the new SOM would renege on modern architecture's social and aesthetic demands, as some small, fashionable architectural firms urged in the early 1980's. That SOM did not do so is a tribute to several young partners who carried SOM into new acts of innovative art charged with social dedication and formal power.

Worry over SOM's continuity and succession rose at a time when faith in American government was unsettled and architects had abandoned Utopian aspirations. Badly torn by riots during demonstrations over civil rights and American presence in Vietnam and Cambodia, American cities in Johnson's late 1960's and Nixon's early 1970's saw violence propel flight from city to suburb. At mid-decade, President Ford refused to aid distressed New York City, and President Carter in 1980 reluctantly promised to rebuild the burned-out Bronx, rescue New York City from insolvency, and improve urban housing, transportation and employment. But California and Massachusetts voted against raising taxes, and the nation elected President Reagan, who promised to reduce governmental functions. In 1982, he defended a multibillion dollar deficit and sharp reductions in urban programs. Americans then did not rally to voices urging better urban dwellings, hospitals or schools. The four conditions SOM had found essential for architectural patronage rarely converged: a society with idealistic objectives; clients who are cultured and altruistic; a respect for craftsmanship; and a reliable economy. As important urban projects were deferred or abandoned, the question was raised: "What is the national agenda? What programs are needed? Where is the demand for architecture?"

7

If, in 1982, America was anxious about military defense and a recessive domestic economy, and called architects only to design office towers and luxury condominiums, then where was the social urgency modern architecture was born to meet? In those circumstances, SOM accepted the only social obligation it was given: to build well, so well, one hoped, that the towers themselves might inspire an urban renaissance. What had eroded was neither modern architects' formal prowess nor their social dedications but society's domestic idealism. Even SOM was limited in how far it might lead a developer towards artistic patronage or press his office tower to benefit an urban neighborhood. Artistic integrity as a way to profit had to be demonstrated every day. Having sharpened their competence on urgent needs at the wartime Oak Ridge Laboratories and postwar Lake Meadows Housing and Air Force Academy [11], SOM sought comparable scope in the 1970's. Early in the decade, SOM addressed important urban problems in plans for Chicago 21, Sacramento's Capitol Area Plan, Oregon's energy studies, the San Antonio River Corridor and the Northeast Railroad Corridor, but the proposals were not sustained by a national imperative.

8
9

Fortunately, the imperative lacking in the American 1970's emerged sporadically in North Africa, the Middle East and Southeast Asia. In 1974–78, SOM designed universities, new towns, airport terminals, and commercial buildings in Algeria, Egypt, Iran, Saudi Arabia, Malaysia, Hong Kong and Peking. Those international projects are epitomized in SOM's Haj Terminal at Jeddah. The exhilaration inherent in planning vital foreign institutions was often accompanied by disappointment over crude construction and cancelled projects. After SOM designed Cairo's Helwan University [12], additional Egyptian work was not stimulated by American investment or the 1979 Egyptian-Israeli treaty. Perhaps the greatest regret surrounds SOM's plans for Iranian cities in 1974–77. After the Shah fled, Khomeini returned and the American Embassy was seized, a religious nationalism halted the Shah's urban and industrial plans. Seeing the Iranian reversal, cautious about fragile foreign economies, suspicious of Soviet Russia's global intentions, and still stung by the disastrous battles in Vietnam and Cambodia, Americans in 1982 watched successive South American, African and Middle Eastern conflicts and debated how much economic or architectural involvement they should risk in foreign causes.

Regrets aside, many SOM partners speak positively of their North African and Middle Eastern experience in 1975. A San Francisco partner recalls that Iranian town planning projects introduced his team to social urgency and primary research into indigenous form. A Chicago partner says that the Algerian university projects "produced a sensitivity to cultural impact." According to Chicago partner Fazlur Khan, "the process of getting into other cultures for the Haj Terminal and University at Makkah made us determined to create form that is rich and sure in its regional origin." In 1975–77, the Haj Terminal drew SOM's New York and Chicago offices together in a search for cultural metaphor, assisted by new technology and computer analysis. If Khomeini's Iran has burned the plans SOM/San Francisco drew for Bandar Shapour, that nation has lost a sensitive vision of a modern city that preserves Islamic tradition.

When they returned to work in the United States in 1976 and 1977, the SOM partners found that American cities were responding to four sources of vitality. First, Canadian and other foreign investors began to build in American cities. Second, American cities

1

10

11

12

13

7 Chase Manhattan Bank, New York, New York.
8 Vinegar plant of the H.J. Heinz Company,
   Pittsburgh, Pennsylvania.
9 John Hancock Center, Chicago, Illinois.
10 Sears Tower, Chicago, Illinois.
11 U.S. Air Force Academy, Colorado Springs
   Colorado.
12 Helwan University, Helwan, Egypt
13 Louise M. Davies Symphony Hall,
   San Francisco, California.

were expanding as financial centers, with burgeoning banking houses, real estate firms, pension funds, insurance companies and brokerage houses, all creating demand for office towers. Third, the financial vitality made cities become places of education and spectacle, with lively markets and cultural institutions. Assisted by small but essential Federal subsidies, theaters, universities, museums, and symphony orchestras now flourished. New York's Metropolitan Museum of Art, later joined by Washington's National Gallery of Art, staged colossal exhibitions that toured nationally. San Francisco opened SOM's Louise M. Davies Symphony Hall [13]; Chicago dedicated SOM's additions to the Art Institute [14]. Then, in a fourth source of urban vitality, many older American cities offered residence close to the financial and professional firms where a now more largely college-educated youth found employment. By 1980, there were 66 million young adults aged 18 to 25, an increase of 30 percent since 1970, and half of them lived in one- or two-person households in metropolitan areas. They increased the demand for rental and later condominium apartments. Although the President's National Urban Policy Report in 1978 identified 123 distressed American cities, those cities that harbored growing financial industries and strong cultural institutions showed a resurgence and now offered a more diversified and extensive range of architectural commissions.

The new urban spirit was intimated as early as 1976. Although America in its post-Vietnam and Watergate years did not then seem to have much to celebrate, its year-long Bicentennial celebration proved otherwise. Far beyond anyone's expectation, the national spectacle cut through disappointment with Nixon and Vietnam, helplessness about cities, and apathy about America's ideals. Suddenly, heritage seemed important. SOM/Washington restored Washington's Mall and designed Constitution Gardens. A rising demand for architectural preservation urged SOM to undertake important restorations: the Paramount Theater in Oakland [15] and Orchestra Hall in Chicago [16]. In Washington, SOM/Washington incorporated two preserved buildings in a new mid-block store at Metropolitan Square. Louis Sullivan's Stock Exchange Trading Room was rebuilt inside SOM's additions to the Chicago Art Institute, and SOM/San Francisco's Crocker Center preserved a classical banking lobby.

Whereas SOM's earlier buildings often declared technological and aesthetic emancipations, preservationism encouraged historic continuities and welcomed context. At the San Francisco Opera House, SOM went so far as to repeat classical masonry forms in reinforced concrete. The classical buildings on either side of San Francisco's new Federal Reserve Building suggested themes that SOM/San Francisco interpreted in the Reserve's Market Street elevation, and SOM/New York's Park Avenue Plaza [17] turns its mass, chamfers its corners, and proportions its bays to accommodate the abutting Racquet and Tennis Club. At 1777 F Street, SOM/Washington incorporated nineteenth-century residential bays in a base for offices terraced above them, and SOM/Chicago's Three First National Plaza adjusts its form to preserved lower buildings. Bassett captured themes in San Francisco's classical Civic Center and banks; SOM/Washington admires Washington's L'Enfant plan and Beaux Arts buildings; and Chicago's Graham proudly emphasizes SOM's faithfulness to the legacy left by Louis H. Sullivan and John Welborn Root. Still, although they are now more willing to seek coherence, even if it means suppressing structural display, SOM did not resort to historical quotation or eclectic reference; they accepted the contextual obligation as part of their more urgent quest for strong modern architecture.

SOM's architecture in 1973–83 also reveals the partnership's response to other changes that swept American society. One was the problem of population dispersal and land consumption. The American population grew from 203 million in 1970 to 226 million in 1980, with about 85 percent of the increase occurring in the West and Southwest. Early in 1973, SOM worked on a statewide plan for California and, later, designed a plan for metropolitan San Antonio in Texas. Open land was being converted to buildings at the rate of one million acres a year, and in 1975, 73 percent of the American people lived in 272 metropolitan regions. Five national preferences guiding such settlements were challenged by SOM in important urban designs and buildings. One preference orders separation of residence from work. A product of early industrial cities, that idea persists in zoning regulations forbidding mixtures of offices and apartments. Such a mixture was pioneered by Chicago's John Hancock Tower, and SOM's new Olympia Centre [18] and One Magnificent Mile offer new combinations. A second idea is that suburban life is preferable, and almost 50 percent of Americans now live in suburbs, with perhaps half of them employed there. SOM's Chicago 21 Plan offers an urban alternative. A third goal establishes the style and scope of American ambition: ownership of the single-family, free-standing house. The apartments in Chicago 21's Dearborn Village offer densities in parklike settings. The fourth preference is the neighborhood vehicular street. That planning premise is challenged in SOM's seminal studies for Irvine Center, San Antonio River Corridor, and Chicago 21, notably its State Street Mall. A fifth and crucial urban premise lies in America's preference for the automobile and truck. SOM planned the bus-pedestrian mall in Portland, Oregon, and proposed an extensive modernization of the Northeast Rail Corridor, starting in Boston and ending in Washington, D.C. SOM also designed subway stations for Cambridge and San Francisco and incorporated transit stations in Minneapolis' Pillsbury Center and Miami's Southeast Financial Center.

14

Another series of studies directed SOM's talents to conservation of open land and forest. Becoming increasingly effective, older conservationist groups, such as the Sierra Club, were now joined by new advocates who saved California's coast north of San Francisco and the Big Sur, where SOM's Nathaniel Owings was a leader. SOM/Portland proposed conservation of islands and waterways in metropolitan areas bordering Oregon's Willamette River. In 1973, when SOM published The California Tomorrow Plan, the Trust for Public Land, urged by the Nature Conservancy, was established to save woodlands, swamps and meadows. The requisite regional planning is demonstrated in SOM's San Antonio River Corridor Study, which proposed water conservation as a means for improving that city's recreational lands and commercial and residential areas.

15

Next, SOM addressed the vexatious problems of buildings bordering highways. Until road construction slowed in the late 1970's, America was making 40,000 miles of road a year and opened much of rural America to development. Consuming land at the rate of 42 acres, each mile of the new Federal highways exposed an additional 2,500 acres to a potential 2,400 houses occupied by 8,500 people in dispersed residential settlements bordered by industry and offices. Until the 1950's, when SOM designed Connecticut General, followed by many fine rural administrative headquarters, builders had few distinguished models. Now in the 1970's, for the Weyerhaeuser Company, on a wooded lakeside outside Tacoma, Washington, SOM/San Francisco designed an internationally admired tier of terraced office floors [19]. 70/90 Universal City Plaza [20] was modelled to ride a slope adjacent to a Los Angeles freeway, and highway-related headquarters were designed for Texaco, General Electric and Westinghouse. A new building type, an office building for a bank's computers, was demonstrated at the Southern California Operations Center for Wells Fargo Bank in El Monte, California. Now SOM also proposed a new regional model for clustered office buildings: Irvine Center, California.

16

The energy crisis brought still other challenges. Beginning with an experimental 1,280-square-foot house in Oregon, SOM/Portland early developed expertise in energy analysis. Such experiments drew attention when even the Alaskan oil flowing from Prudhoe Bay beginning in June 1977 could not meet energy needs if consumption was not curtailed. Seeking a State policy for alternates to oil for producing electricity, Oregon's Governor in 1973 commissioned SOM/Portland to study nuclear and hydroelectric power. SOM's study showed that strong conservation measures could reduce reliance on oil and nuclear generation. Failure in Pennsylvania's Three Mile Island nuclear plant prompted the antinuclear demonstration at Washington in 1979, and coal still remained the primary source of electricity in 1982. By then, oil was plentiful again, as supplies increased and America stabilized its rate of consumption. Meanwhile, energy economies sparked four architectural responses: compact massing that reduces exposed surfaces; improved insulation and cladding; lessened dependence on lamps and motors; and improved cycling of cooled or heated air. The first response led to the cubic massing and internal atria in SOM/Chicago's 33 West Monroe Street in Chicago [21] and Pan American Life Center in New Orleans [22]. The second response brought smaller panes of thermal glass and larger use of masonry walls, after Italian quarriers perfected their sawing and polishing of thin granite slabs. Those features are visible in SOM/San Francisco's InterFirst Plaza in Houston [23] and Crocker Center in San Francisco. The third response is evident in the atria, double-story elevators and task lighting of 33 West Monroe Street. The fourth is essential to SOM/Denver's Gulf Mineral Resources Company buildings outside Denver. An experiment combining aspects of all

17

14 Art Institute of Chicago, Chicago, Illinois.
15 Paramount Theater, Oakland, California.
16 Orchestra Hall, Chicago, Illinois.
17 Park Avenue Plaza, New York, New York.

1

18

18 Olympia Centre, Chicago, Illinois.
19 Weyerhaeuser Headquarters, Tacoma,
Washington.
20 70/90 Universal City Plaza, Universal City,
California.

19

20

four responses is the office building SOM/New York designed for the Prudential Insurance Company outside Princeton, New Jersey.

As energy costs rose, inflation itself directly affected architecture. With construction costs more than tripled since 1960, inflation favored office towers that promised rental income. Costs also decreed that a city's open or underutilized land, including its parking lots, would remain vacant until private investors could gamble on a building's profitable return. Difficulties in assembling capital often caused long delays between a building's conception and erection. With plans completed in 1973, SOM/San Francisco's 444 Market Street ran against the economic slump of 1974 and 1975 and only after the Shaklee Company became its prime tenant could construction start towards 444's opening in 1981.

Rapid design was required to attract investors' funds, gain approval for plans, erect buildings, and realize rental income to carry the high cost of borrowed funds. Few architectural firms were ready to respond to clients' need for alternative schemes and speedy cost analysis. When capital was ready, construction drawings were wanted quickly, and rising costs demanded flexible, economical structural systems, notably the perimetal columnar, or tube, structures in high-rise towers, where SOM led the way. Steel might be more costly than concrete but quicker to erect, or the reverse, depending on the time and place. In 1981, the deep granite window frames SOM/New York proposed for a tall building in Canada were eliminated to save costs. Rarely did SOM now have the luxury of modelled surfaces and deep reveals, as in Houston's earlier Tenneco Building or San Francisco's Alcoa Building. Instead, graphic composition in flamed and polished granite appears in San Francisco's Crocker Center, and a pattern of white and black granites ornaments Miami's Southeast Financial Center.

Although general inflation and energy costs affected architecture, technology itself was not greatly advanced beyond what was current in the late 1960's. Versatile structural tubes gave more flexible, lighter construction in tall buildings, eased the fitting of buildings to irregular sites, and accommodated combinations of office, commercial and residential spaces. Improved tinted and mirrored glass introduced varieties of translucency and opaqueness, often in combination. Where manufacturers could not eliminate ripples from double glazed windows, architects might choose to seek overall shimmering surfaces, as in SOM/New York's Park Avenue Plaza. Although the astronautical explorations stimulated invention, direct architectural dividends were minimal, limited to miniaturized electronic equipment, new alloys and new fabrics, but, indirectly, space exploration hastened the development of computer analysis, which held much architectural promise.

SOM early saw its potential. Installing an IBM 1620 in 1963, SOM set it to analyzing structural design. That ambitious goal became increasingly important, and while administrative data about man-hours and costs, materials, and furnishings were being computerized, SOM developed the computer's graphic potential. Duplicating floor plans, with detailed structure, ducts, wiring, pipes and furniture, was achieved with improved computers and staff by 1976. Next came rapid and accurate computer analysis of alternate building configurations, structural systems, energy demands, and building materials. By 1980, computerized graphic representations enabled SOM's architects to analyze multiple perspectives of New York's Irving Trust Operations Center and transverse sections through Chicago's 33 West Monroe Street. In 1981, SOM's computers could display downtown Denver, Chicago, New York and Los Angeles in three-dimensional views, and buildings SOM proposed could be inserted in scale and studied from many angles. The computer showed the tower of Chicago's Three First National Plaza in its urban setting, documented year-round hourly incidence of sun on its nine-story atrium, and drew its structure and atrium trusses. Computer graphics revealed the shadows to be cast by Chicago's One Magnificent Mile, helped with the analysis of the tubular frame carrying Houston's Allied Bank, and drew the complexly curved form of Jeddah's Haj tents [24, 25]. For Denver's Gulf Mineral Resources buildings, a computer solved 72 equations simultaneously on an hour-by-hour basis to predict energy efficiencies. SOM's adventurous and costly development of computerized representations is a signal and growing contribution to architects and clients.

Central to its technical and social response to the currents affecting American society was SOM's concern for aesthetic quality. Beyond the decisions needed daily in studio discussions of a building's form, there was rising inquiry into modern architecture's premises. In 1981, a conference in New York City confronted SOM/New York's design partners with challenges made by architects who, claiming to be "post-modernists," criticized SOM's attitudes about functionalism, structural expression and technological imagery. Critics often cited directions SOM had taken in the 1960's, like SOM/Chicago's John Hancock Tower, but neglected new directions in SOM/Houston's Allied Bank, SOM/New York's Park Avenue Plaza, SOM/Chicago's One Magnificent Mile, or the even more dramatic departures in SOM/San Francisco's California First Bank and Federal Reserve Building. Some SOM partners themselves held reservations about isolated, tall office towers and doubted that Chicago's 4.5-million-square-foot Sears Tower should enter 25,000 people through a mere revolving door. SOM's recent buildings were neither abstractions nor uncaring about urban and historic context, but SOM's critics wanted more. Many rejected early modern architecture's measures of efficiency, economy and mechanism. One writer blamed the liberal social goals of Walter Gropius, conveniently omitting the Saarinens and Bunshafts who did not share them but were modernists nonetheless. What the post-modernists wanted was never clear. Sometimes they fashioned shiny worlds of exposed machinery, ornamented facades with whimsical stylistic quotations, and manipulated masses and voids to butt contrasted scales. Their debates were not nearly as profound as those that ushered modern architecture into the American 1930's, an earlier decade when building slackened and theorists flourished.

However entertaining, those discussions did not deflect SOM from its aesthetic heritage. Even though the diversity of SOM's buildings in the early 1980's made it increasingly difficult to define any unifying theme, perhaps most partners still agree with the late Fazlur Khan's statement, "Technology is our art form." Proud of the Haj Terminal, Khan urged the marriage of technical support, sculptural form and spatial sequence so that their unity looks simple and inevitable. A tower's form, he believed, should originate from spaces formed by a structure that integrates all technology. He was enthusiastic about the tall building: "It gives work and residential space when and where most needed." Its scale and density excited him: "The tall building is a remarkable economic and symbolic success." When he recited the history of structure, how the steel beam and column frame led to shear wall construction, then to framed tubes, next to tubes within tubes, and ultimately to a cluster of tubes, as in the Sears Tower, Khan presented technology as a great urban service. Thus, the tube structures enabling One Magnificent Mile and the Olympia Centre to combine work space with residential space are admirable for their social service. That is one part of SOM's heritage: Structure's functional purpose is social.

For SOM structural expression has a further meaning, as Khan also insisted. Not satisfied by a form's sheerly mechanical or social performance, SOM has sought to make structure symbolic. Here the arcade at San Francisco's Federal Reserve Bank and the towers grouped at Chicago's One Magnificent Mile suggest the structural origins of great historic symbols, such as the Egyptian hypostyle hall, the Grecian colonnade, the Roman basilica, and the Gothic cathedral. There, the structural element is organized for symbolic intent: Doric column becomes Grecian order and medieval pier becomes Gothic bay. Unlike Wright and Sullivan who adopted organic metaphors, SOM premises order and meaning on nature conceived as a well-working machine. Since the machine itself provides escape from servitude to utility's literal expression, modern mechanistic forms soon subordinated function and organized themselves to express mechanism as symbol. Electric motors freed tall buildings to disregard natural ventilation, illumination, and contiguities among occupants. Machines released mechanistic form from functional fidelity. Form could seek its own geometric perfection and celebrate technology's precision, economy and luster. The efficient or funicular shape became symbolic, a mechanism denoting economy, logic, even reliability and progress, which, in emulation of earlier corporate patrons, the aggressive developer-client now wanted to declare.

Surrounding developers' zeal to build prestigious buildings was a rising fervor to build in urban financial and commercial districts. Foreign investors saw opportunity early, as highlighted in the 1976 purchase by Toronto's Olympia & York of eight New York City skyscrapers for $350 million, said to be worth over $1 billion in 1982. Pleased to encourage such private investors, cities awarded tax abatements, extra floor areas and other relief from zoning restrictions, in exchange for public gardens, retail lobbies and enclosed entries to subways. Given a location at a major transit interchange and allowed

21

22

23

24

25

maximum net floor area, the rentable office tower was profitable in a rising market, and foreign and, then later, American speculative builders risked expensive capital. Their bold decisions to invest in American high-rise office buildings beginning in 1976 resulted in energetic construction during 1979–83. As their buildings rose, the American economy was still depressed in the three influential sectors of housing, automobiles, and heavy manufacturing. Thus, although 1982 and 1983 saw the completion of many of SOM's finest office towers, a lessening demand for office space slowed new investments. Some foreign developers encountered reverses and sold the American properties they had avidly bought or financed in 1976, and the sporadic opportunities for new tall office towers in 1982 and early 1983 did not match those boldly offered in 1976–81, when developers in that five-year span quickened the vitality of American cities.

SOM had enjoyed early successes in gaining admirable architecture through developers. As early as the 1960's, with Harry Helmsley in association with Morse-Diesel, SOM had designed the lower Manhattan tower that Helmsley later partly leased to Marine Midland Bank, and, in Buffalo, SOM had designed the Marine Midland Center for a developer, Cabot, Cabot and Forbes, and a banking group led by Seymour Knox. Even the best developers demanded adherence to restrictive confines. Building sites were apt to be irregular, and parcels were won or lost as design proceeded. Chicago's Three First National Plaza reflects the need to preserve views and a historic Chicago building. New York's Irving Trust, Atlanta's Georgia-Pacific and Washington's Metro Center had to adjust their forms to suit special sites. Programs that required mixing rental offices, retail stores, and banking floors, sometimes adding residential apartments, tended to be complex and conflicting: maximum rental area but ample windows and views; slender mechanical cores but speedy elevator service; privacy and security in office floors but easy public access to retail areas. Then, too, each tall office tower represented an investment of $100 million or more, plus the costs of financing, and its investors wanted rapid occupancy. Since they often represented banks, insurance companies and pension funds, the investors' multiple voices could affect a tower's program and quality. Nor were they the final hazard: rental occupants at Park Avenue Plaza introduced alien ceiling lights, furniture and partitions, in marked contrast to SOM's experience at Lever House and Inland Steel.

Still, SOM's developer buildings often achieve architectural distinction. Fisher Brothers' Park Avenue Plaza has won New Yorkers' admiration not only for its counterpoint to the classic Racquet and Tennis Club but for opening Park Avenue to the wider midblock scale. Into the class of its signal Tenneco Building, SOM now introduced two developer's buildings: Houston's InterFirst Plaza and Allied Bank, with the possibility of Campeau Tower and Four Houston Center ahead. Chicago's masterpieces – Inland Steel, Brunswick, John Hancock and Sears Tower – now had allies in Three First National Plaza and One Magnificent Mile. California gained the two Crocker Centers in San Francisco and Los Angeles. Their artistic merit disguises the persistence needed in urging perfected detail, even where a contest came down to a quarter-inch recess or almost imperceptible subtleties within a palette of granite, glass and metal.

SOM's architecture might be displayed in any of several sequences: by building type, by chronology, by individual offices, or by regional folios. The regional sequence has been chosen for this book because it reflects SOM's geographic presence. Accordingly, SOM's American buildings are presented in four folios; a fifth shows the international work. Underlying the prefatory themes introducing each folio are the national economic, social and aesthetic issues that affected SOM's architectural response in the difficult, often adverse and sometimes triumphant decade, 1973–83.

21 33 West Monroe Street, Chicago, Illinois.
22 Pan American Life Center, New Orleans,
   Louisiana.
23 InterFirst Plaza, Houston, Texas.
24 Georgia-Pacific Center, Atlanta, Georgia.
25 Crocker Center and Galleria,
   San Francisco, California.

2

3

4

5

The West Coast

Is there a Western mind, some regional character in California's Bay Area or Washington's Puget Sound, that calls for distinctive architecture? Merely to raise that question sounded quaint as early as 1960. Much earlier, Western regionalism had excited architect Winsor Soule to imagine a Spanish style for Santa Barbara, and indigenous residential wooden forms still intrigued architects in the 1960's, even while the West Coast was losing its regional outlook and landscapes. Commercial, industrial and housing developments spread to valleys and mountainsides, and "Cry California!" was the plea that opened the West Coast's 1970's. It lamented problems that lie beyond the scope of regionalists' inquiry.

SOM/San Francisco led a forceful drive for planned regional growth. Encouraged by founding partner Nathaniel Owings, a leader in conserving Big Sur, SOM in 1971 prepared a California-wide model for conservation, the California Tomorrow Plan. Earlier, SOM had demonstrated a compact rural community in California's Carmel Valley Manor [2], and SOM's Mauna Kea Hotel [3] graces a beautiful shoreline in Hawaii.

SOM/San Francisco further developed its planning concepts in three seminal documents. For California's Napa Valley towns, whose vineyards were invaded by housing developments, SOM in 1974 showed how Saint Helena might improve its approaches, circulation, building lots and Main Street. In 1977, Sacramento received SOM's design for 75 acres of prime downtown land which had been cleared and turned into paved parking lots in the 1960's. For a triangular site created by three freeways at Irvine, SOM in 1981 planned a grid street plan and tall office buildings with plazas and gardens. Approached from elevated freeways, Irvine Center promised to become an attractive land-saving, commercially successful alternative to strip highway sprawl.

In Oregon, partner David Pugh lead SOM/Portland, which earlier designed the Portland Center [4]. Later joined by James Christensen, SOM guided a reorganization of the downtown business district. The Tri-Met Mall [5] is often cited for its successful recapture of centralized shopping within a metropolitan region. SOM/San Francisco prepared a design for Advanced Micro Devices, which contains trapezoidal garden courtyards and an entrance past a polished green marble slab bearing AMD's logo. SOM/San Francisco dramatized the Southern California Operations Center of Wells Fargo Bank at

6

7

8

1 Skyline of San Francisco, California.
2 Carmel Valley Manor, Carmel Valley, California.
3 Mauna Kea Beach Hotel, Kamuela, Hawaii.
4 Portland Center, Portland, Oregon.
5 Tri-Met Mall, Portland, Oregon.
6 Wells Fargo Southern California Operations Center, El Monte, California.
7 Bank of America, San Francisco, California.
8 Crown Zellerbach Building, San Francisco, California.

9

10
11

1

El Monte [6]: a triangular prism connected to a block devoted to computer operations. Ranging from regional plan to high-rise office buildings, SOM/San Francisco's work served an important clientele throughout the West Coast and, in the 1970's, attracted commissions in eastern states and in Europe, the Middle East and Southeast Asia. Opened in 1946 by founding partner Nathaniel Owings, the office soon gained two of its current administrative partners, John O. Merrill in 1949 and Walter Costa the following year. Merrill, who is the son of SOM's late founding partner, attributes the office's initial brilliance to Edward C. Basseft, who, joining SOM from Eero Saarinen's office in 1955, has created most of SOM/San Francisco's distinctive buildings. Fully founded in his craft but also inventive and whimsical, Bassett early sensed the formal, classical tone of San Francisco's financial leaders, and his architectural talent attracted designers Marc Goldstein in 1961 and Lawrence Doane in 1968. By 1982, those three design partners could count almost two dozen major buildings in San Francisco alone, where SOM, with associated firms, designed the celebrated Bank of America, built in 1969–71. Until the Bank of America Headquarters [7], San Francisco was not avid about modern form in its downtown financial and commercial districts. Following its 1906 earthquake, San Francisco had been rebuilt predominantly with classical buildings: The Italianate Pacific Union Club and Fairmont Hotel, the Roman downtown banks, Bernard Maybeck's Fine Arts Palace, and Arthur Brown Jr.'s Opera House and City Hall. An ardent and skillful practitioner, Timothy Pfleuger, at 450 Sutter, made Aztec and Mayan ornament enhance an otherwise classical composition. Willis Polk's glazed and metallic Hallidie Building and Frank Lloyd Wright's later Morris Store were considered to be aberrations from classical success, as was the previously cited Bay Regional style. The Miesian or "Eastern" aspect of SOM's early U.S. Naval Station at Monterey and SOM's Crown Zellerbach [8] and Alcoa Buildings [9] in San Francisco did not lessen resistance to modern architecture. Then, about 1957, Bassett drew upon classical references for the John Hancock Building [10]. Still San Franciscans withheld enthusiasm. At that point the Bank of America Headquarters [11] added a new dimension to lingering classicism and regionalism, winning international respect.

While earning its current eminence, SOM/San Francisco completed four outstanding projects: the Oakland-Alameda stadium and arena [12]; the Laney College campus [13], the Carmel

9 Alcoa Building, San Francisco, California.
10 John Hancock Building, San Francisco, California.
11 Bank of America, San Francisco, California.
12 Oakland-Alameda County Coliseum, Oakland, California.
13 Laney College, Oakland, California.
14 Carmel Valley Manor, Carmel Valley, California.
15 Weyerhaeuser Headquarters, Tacoma, Washington.

12

13

14
15

16

17

18

19

Valley Manor [14], and the Weyerhaeuser Company Headquarters outside Tacoma [15]. Like another superb example, SOM's Mauna Kea Hotel in Hawaii [16], all are admirable for their strong massing, harmonious fit to site, rich elaboration of form, and sculptured spatial sequences. The success with Weyerhaeuser led to SOM/San Francisco's being recalled in the 1970's to design Weyerhaeuser's new research center at Tacoma.

In Los Angeles, long hospitable to modern architecture, SOM developed a strong presence in the 1970's with both SOM/Los Angeles, led by partner Richard Ciceri, and SOM/San Francisco working there. For a sloped site between two highways, SOM/San Francisco's Goldstein modeled low, terraced office buildings for the Music Corporation of America at 70/90 Universal City Plaza [17], and, on a previously disarrayed site in Santa Monica, SOM/Los Angeles partner Maris Peika installed Santa Monica's First Federal Savings and Loan Association in a terraced twelve-story building whose dark gray glass ribbons and deeply channelled concrete walls shape a fine plaza [18]. Investing heavily to concentrate financial and commercial activity, Los Angeles encouraged banking headquarters, convention-sized hotels and national companies to build tall buildings around Bunker Hill. There, abutting multilevel, interlaced freeways, SOM's Crocker Center [19] rises in two towers, each trapezoidal in plan, set perpendicular to each other. Polished granite and bronze-glazed, the towers designed by Goldstein dominate the core with tall angled planes and knife-edge corners. As the Crocker Center opened with prestigious tenants in 1982, hopes were stirred for filling the emptiness in downtown Los Angeles.

Still, the Bay Area is where SOM has made its greatest mark on the West Coast. Important urban space has been entrusted to SOM. When the Bay Area Rapid Transit was extended across the Bay from Oakland-Berkeley to San Francisco, SOM prepared BART's underground stations for Powell and Montgomery Streets [20], finished in 1972. The proposed Transbay Terminal [21] is intended to be a glazed, multilevel interchange for passengers transferring between buses. At the hinge joining San Francisco's retail and financial districts, SOM's Crocker Center [22] contributes a three-story enclosed shopping arcade, and SOM's Five Fremont Center [23] rises from a retail courtyard. At 45 Fremont Street, SOM's newest Bechtel Building springs its 30- and 40-foot steel frame bays from a broad terrace, and, while 444 Market Street [24], completed in 1981, will be remembered

20

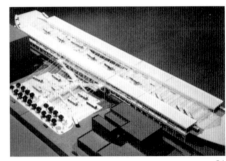

21

22

16 Mauna Kea Beach Hotel, Kamuela, Hawaii.
17 70/90 Universal City Plaza, Universal City, California.
18 First Federal Square, Santa Monica, California.
19 Crocker Center, Los Angeles, California.
20 BART station at Montgomery Street, San Francisco, California.
21 Transbay Terminal, San Francisco, California.
22 Crocker Center and Galleria, San Francisco, California.

23

24
25

for its silver-anodized aluminum skyline terraces, its groundline serrations and sidewalk setbacks make a greater urban gift. Added to SOM's concern for San Francisco's urban spaces is great care for its architectural heritage. Urged by Edgar Kaiser and Stephen Bechtel, SOM restored Oakland's Paramount Theater [25], a 1931 cinema, to its splendor of colored velvets, exuberant lighting and stylized lily, tulip and scimitar ornament. At the Crocker Center in San Francisco, SOM plans to remove the banal existing tower but preserve its fine banking hall, which will support an outdoor roof garden, adjacent to the new Crocker tower. For the Civic Center, designed in the 1920's by the talented classicist Arthur Brown Jr., SOM succeeded in making new buildings relate successfully to their important neighbors. The addition to the Opera House [26] repeats its classical forms, and the proposed State Office Building bears compositional themes in neighboring buildings and aligns its interior court on a diagonal to City Hall. That focus also set the orientation for the Louise M. Davies Symphony Hall [27], which, on a tight site, develops an acoustically vibrant 3,000-seat auditorium within a building that offers grace notes to the Civic Center's classicism.

The rare imagination that creates modern images which harmonize with classical settings appears again in San Francisco's California First Bank, completed in 1977, and the Federal Reserve Building [28] completed in early 1983. Unmistakably the artful work of SOM's Bassett, California First Bank [29] offsets its service core and stretches long spans between columns to open a glazed banking lobby to vistas towards the colonnade of the 1908 Bank of California. Smooth and textured precast concrete (probably the best any architect has summoned) carries to the roofline where the twelve columns' tips reappear in an echo of function and articulated joinery. In the Federal Reserve, his most recent building in San Francisco, Bassett refused to succumb to a prosaic program and stepped a broad eight-story building in two-story increments over a four-story base. Recessed from Market Street, the facade marries themes in neighboring classical buildings, and the loggia is a deft triumph of structure serving as symbol. Thus, in its extensive, multiple Western presence, SOM demonstrated models of conservation, preservation, office and residential development, integrated transportation systems, high-rise office buildings, places for cultural assembly, and symbols of government – all admirable responses to the cries for rescuing the splendid but endangered West Coast.

26

27

28
29

23 Five Fremont Center, San Francisco, California.
24 444 Market Street, San Francisco, California.
25 Paramount Theater, Oakland, California.
26 Addition to the San Francisco Opera House, San Francisco, California.
27 Louise M. Davies Symphony Hall, San Francisco, California.
28 The Federal Reserve Bank of San Francisco, California.
29 The California First Bank, San Francisco, California.

The California First Bank
San Francisco, California

The site of this 23-story office tower, completed in 1977, is a 19,000-square-foot corner in the city's financial district. The client required a headquarters building that could provide adequate space for its own needs, including a major banking hall, as well as prestige office space for tenants.

While the tower is free-standing on three sides, the fourth side is joined to an adjacent party wall by means of a recessed link element. This is an offset core which contains seven passenger elevators arranged in two banks, as well as a service elevator and utility spaces on the tower floor levels. The tower lobby entrance is at the podium level of the core with a ramp down at the rear for truck delivery, executive parking and service areas. Offsetting the core achieved unencumbered office floors for maximum flexibility and efficiency, and more important, enabled the podium level of the tower to be devoted entirely to the banking hall.

The steel frame structure is clad with precast concrete units composed of a matrix of white cement and Sierra white granite aggregate, the most common granite in use throughout San Francisco. Contrasting horizontal bands of smoothly cast and of heavily sandblasted surfaces make up the spandrel panels. The plinth, entry porch and steps are of the same stone. On the tower facades, a frameless glazing system of $\frac{3}{8}$-inch-thick solar gray glass is set flush between spandrel panels and the round tower columns. On the uppermost executive floor level, glazing is recessed behind the columns and the spandrel line in order to achieve a strong shadow at the top of the building.

The 23-story office tower occupies a prominent corner site in downtown San Francisco.

Access from the street to the high banking hall ▷ (to the left) is from a podium level. The tower lobby is located in a recessed link between the tower and an existing party wall.

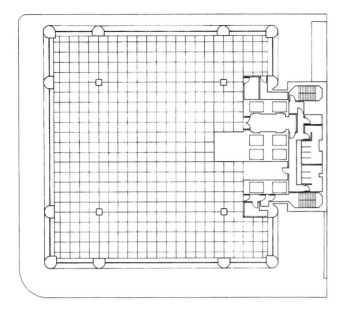

Plans (street level, mezzanine level, typical floor).

The tower seen from the west. An expression ▷
of classical building elements was achieved
within a contemporary architectural vocabulary.

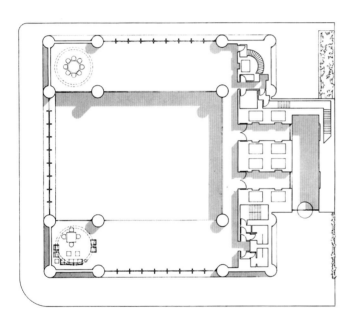

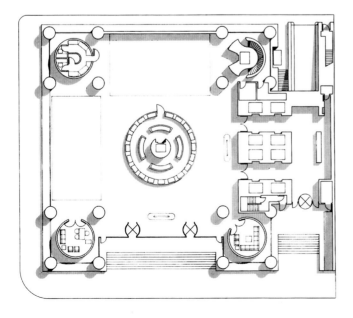

444 Market Street
San Francisco, California

The site of this 36-story office tower, completed in 1980, abuts the strong diagonal of Market Street, San Francisco's major avenue. To the north, a party wall is shared with an adjacent structure, and the two remaining sides are aligned with the normal city grid. Working within the economic restrictions of normal rental office patterns and the geometry of the site, the elevation along Market Street has a sawtooth shape, while core elements such as elevators and other vertical services are grouped along the party wall to the north. This results in five desirable corner offices along the tower's most important side and provides floors of about 19,000 square feet for flexible subdivision. At the top of the tower on the east side, the building steps back at the 33rd, 34th and 35th floors, permitting office spaces to open out on extensively planted terraces protected by windscreens.

Between the tower and an adjacent building to the west, a two-story wing defines a small plaza, an extension of the adjacent Mechanics' Monument Plaza. The principal entrance to the tower lobby is from this space. The lobby is treated as an arcade leading to the street to the east. The lobbies of three elevator banks, including 16 passenger elevators and one freight elevator, open into it, as do the adjacent rental areas.

The tower has a welded steel moment frame with lightweight concrete fill on metal deck floors. The curtain wall is an aluminum stick system with insulated spandrel panels in anodized silver used in conjunction with ⅜-inch tinted gray glazing. The air-conditioned building is fully sprinklered for fire protection. Individual floor control capability with fan rooms on every third floor was provided to save energy through close adaption to user needs.

Section.

The tower rises from a tree-lined open space ▷ which is a visual enlargement of Mechanics' Monument Plaza on Market Street.

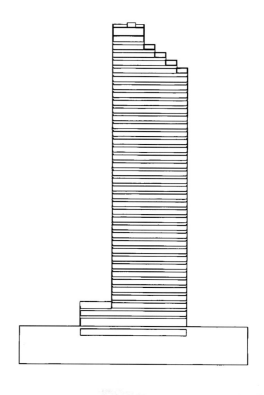

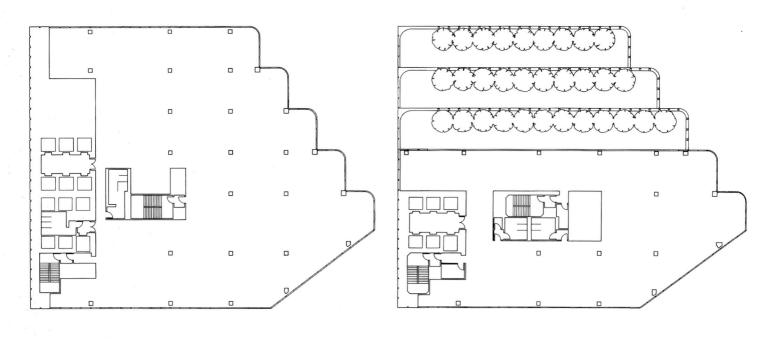

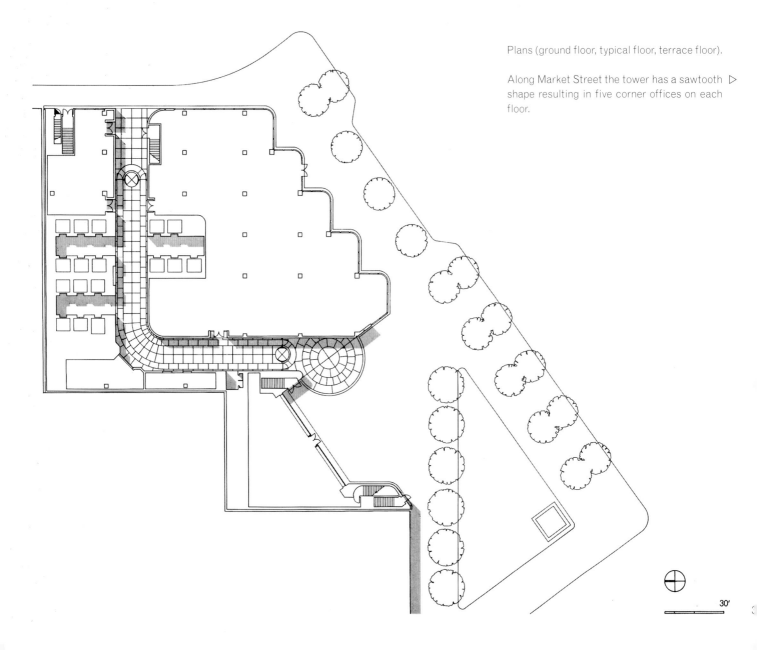

Plans (ground floor, typical floor, terrace floor).

Along Market Street the tower has a sawtooth ▷
shape resulting in five corner offices on each
floor.

30′

45 Fremont Street (Bechtel Building)
San Francisco, California

The Bechtel Corporation headquarters building, constructed in San Francisco in 1967 for this engineering and building enterprise, had become too small to provide the space needed in the early seventies. Overflow departments had to be located in a new structure located on an adjacent site. The small size of the site required a highly economical building shape and a flush exterior skin.

The dimensions of the tower, 150 feet by 120 feet, were the maximum allowed by the San Francisco Planning Code. The building has an area of 780,000 gross square feet. A small planted plaza is shared by both the original building and the new structure. They also share the provision of access to rapid transit on the site.

The steel moment frame structure rests on pile foundations and has five bays of 30 feet in the long direction as well as three bays of 40 feet on the short side. An oblong, centrally placed interior core, containing elevators, staircases and restrooms allows the interior planning to use flexible partitioning. Connections to the original building are made below grade and by a glazed sky-bridge.

The elevation design clearly reflects the long spans of the structural system. Aluminum spandrel members of up to 40 feet in length were prefabricated and installed in one piece. The building was one of the first projects with such an aluminum skin to receive a matt paint finish which is light beige in color. Windows are formed by 10-foot sections of monolithic bronze-tinted glass and are set into the aluminum skin with but a minimal difference between closed and glazed surfaces. The street level entrance is finished in a travertine-clad core and exterior brick paving.

Plan (typical floor).

The facade clearly reflects the long spans of ▷ the steel structural system.

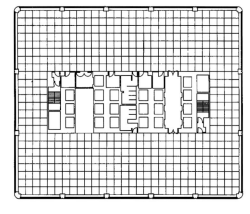

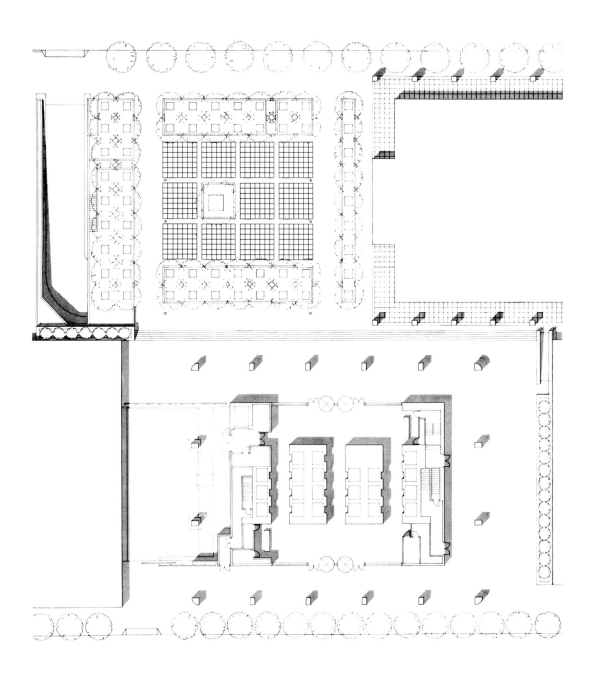

30'

◁ Plan (ground level).

View of the pedestrian plaza between the 1967 headquarters building and the new tower.

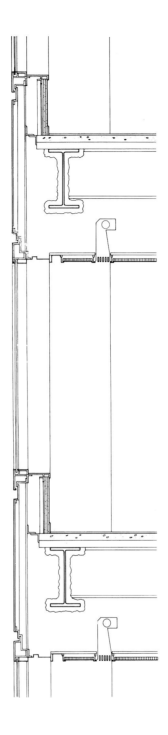

Facade detail. Windows are formed by 10-foot sections of monolithic bronze-tinted glass, which are set into the aluminum skin with minimal difference between closed and glazed surfaces.

The travertine-clad core and the brick-paved ▷ landscaped plaza contribute towards a pleasant pedestrian environment.

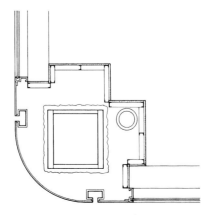

Five Fremont Center
San Francisco, California

The site is situated at the edge of the financial district south of Market Street, San Francisco's main business artery, facing the Transbay Regional Bus Terminal. This central location, convenient to all traffic systems, led to the creation of two new pedestrian paths across the site. These paths are formed by the residual spaces between two low retail structures and the 43-story tower. The entire complex is woven together at street level by a consistently patterned series of facades, colonnades and arcades.

The tower rises 600 feet, given identity by sawtooth corner setbacks of increasing depth, set within continuous seams of vertical bay windows. Employing these rather minor variations in shape, a convincing design is created with strong vertical emphasis. In addition, a large number of desirable corner offices are provided, especially at the top of the tower.

The steel structure of the tower portion is developed as a tube system with perimeter columns at 15 feet on center, deep column-free office areas and a classic central structural core. The exterior walls are clad with travertine panels and silver-colored reflective glass.

Plan (typical floor).

The tower was given identity by minor varia- ▷
tions of its basically rectangular plan.

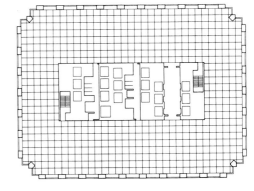

Plan (ground level).

Tower elevation and section of the two-story ▷
retail arcade.

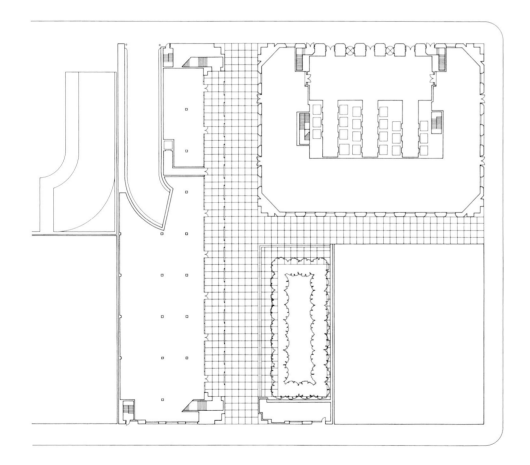

60'

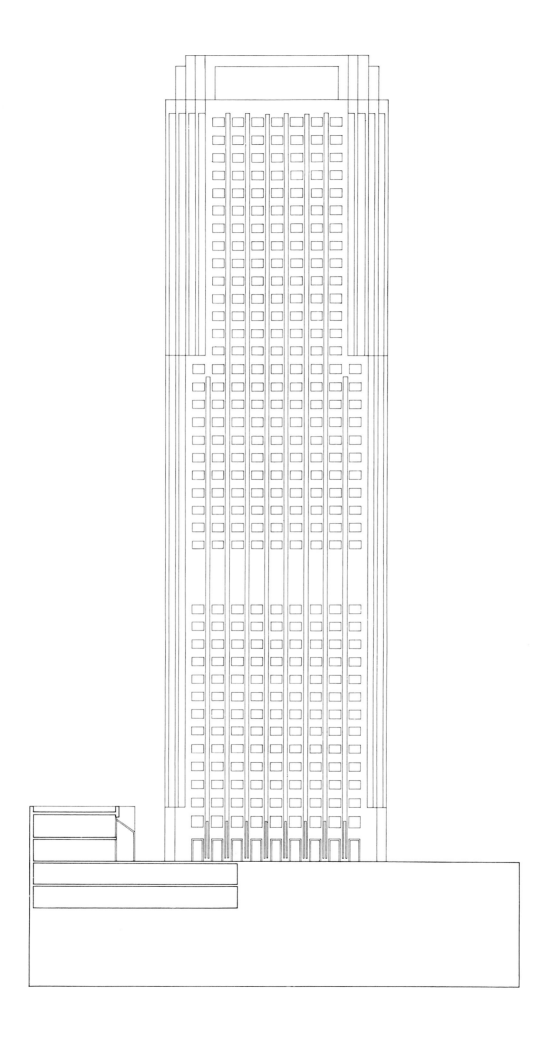

41

The Federal Reserve Bank of San Francisco
San Francisco, California

The site of The Federal Reserve Bank is nearly an entire city block on the south side of Market Street, at its eastern end near the waterfront, and at that point where California Street (San Francisco's second most important street) intersects Market. It is flanked by two handsome, older commercial structures: The Southern Pacific Building to the east and the Pacific Gas and Electric (PG&E) Building to the west.

The program of some two-thirds of a million square feet is complex, including traditional office building functions and services, public exhibit and educational facilities, and highly technical accommodations for the movement, storage and recording of large amounts of currency.

The design solution is a building which extends the full length of the block to a height of eight stories, striking a balance between its lower neighbor to the east and the higher one to the west. The facade steps back slightly in two-story increments permitting the handsome upper story and cornice treatments of the neighbors to be seen effectively. The wall treatment is restrained, employing granite in two finishes, applied horizontally in concert with the strip windows. The stone color harmonizes with the brick of one neighbor and the enamelled window frames, setback railings and other metal parts are colored to match the accents of the other.

The building is set back from Market Street in order to permit the introduction of a pedestrian loggia, or porch, for the full block as an open colonnade. It is a separate structure, treated differently in detail and material, related purposely in scale and rhythms to the base of its neighbors and to the details and materials of newly reconstructed Market Street.

The loggia is designed to receive intensive and large-scale planting for its full length, including a variety of full-size trees and large shrubs. The intent is to create a memorable architectural and landscape incident at an important place in the city.

The freestanding pedestrian loggia fronting Market Street.

View of the complex across Market Street. ▷

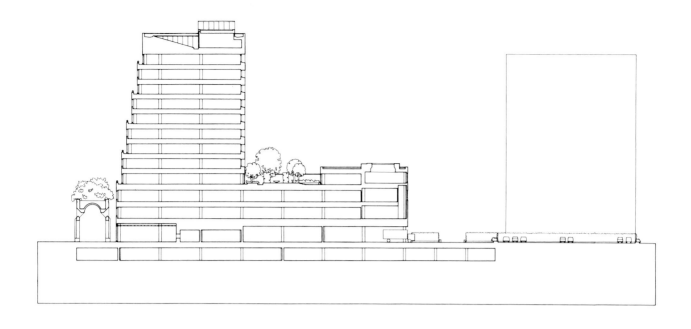

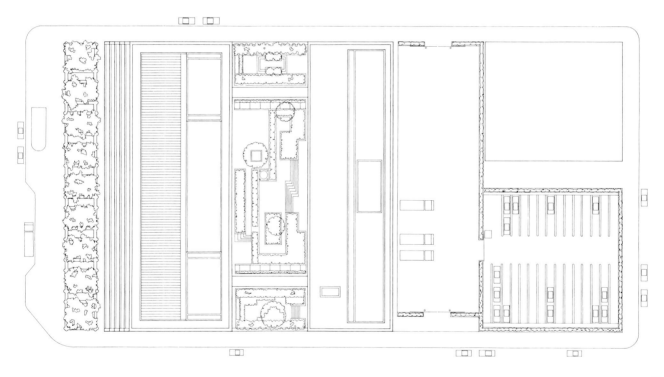

60'

46

◁ Site plan and section.

The facade of the office block is substantially set back from Market Street, permitting the rich ornamentation of its two handsome neighbors to be seen effectively.

Along Market Street the loggia creates pedestrian scale and establishes an important element of continuity.

Crocker Center and Galleria
San Francisco, California

The client is a major West Coast bank, on an important site located at the juncture of the retail and financial districts. A portion of the site has been occupied by the institution for many years. The master plan called for construction of a new office tower and a block-long retail galleria, followed by the removal of the bank's present offices above its banking hall, and finally the restoration of the hall and installation of a garden upon its roof.

The focus of the complex is the open-ended, three-level retail galleria, covered by a large glazed vault. The galleria joins two important retail streets and also connects the new 38-story office tower with the existing banking hall, providing a variety of new pedestrian movements at a significant point in the city. The property slopes strongly down from west to east, permitting the tower lobby to coincide with the mid-level of the galleria, and the lower level of the galleria to the banking hall. The tower lobby is pushed to the rear, permitting shops to occupy the street edge at the bottom of the tower.

Renovation of the banking hall will improve pedestrian flow, but will otherwise be limited to careful enhancement and restoration of the existing traditional interior. After demolition of the tower above, elevators will carry the public to the new garden on the roof.

Above the specialized shopfront treatment at street level, the tower walls are a skin of stone and reflective glass. The stone is a warm colored granite from Texas in a pattern of polished and thermal finishes, reflecting the structural frame behind, with the glass set flush in a minimum frame. Window washing equipment will be engaged by a pattern of stainless steel studs that project from the wall.

The tower is framed as a steel tube with a 12-foot module at the exterior wall. The office floors are 20,180 square feet in area and are column free. The floors are fully electrified steel deck with concrete fill. The building is completely air conditioned and incorporates the latest life safety techniques.

Plan (typical floor).

Plan (ground level). ▷

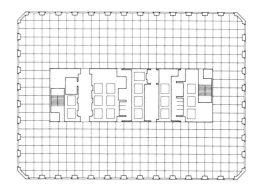

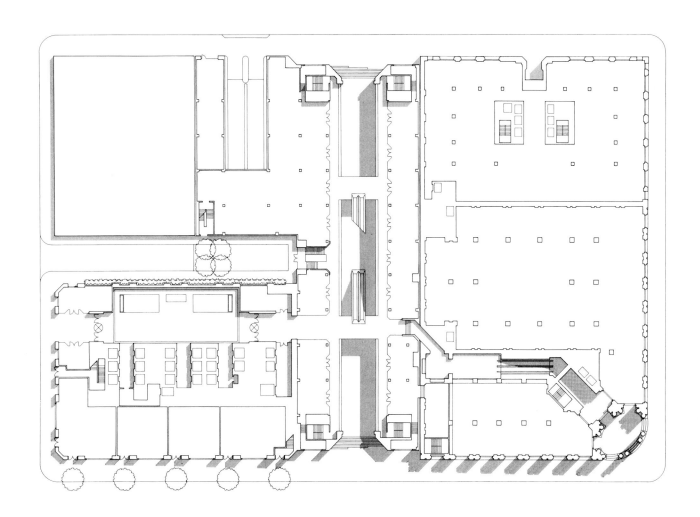

60'

Section through the galleria. Where the various parts and functions of the complex meet, the three-story glass-vaulted retail galleria creates a significant pedestrian axis.

The galleria seen from the south with the new ▷ tower to the west.

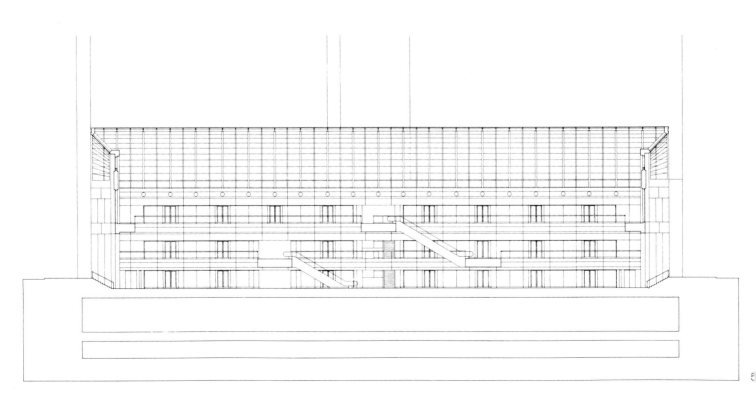

South elevation.

Interior view of the galleria. ▷

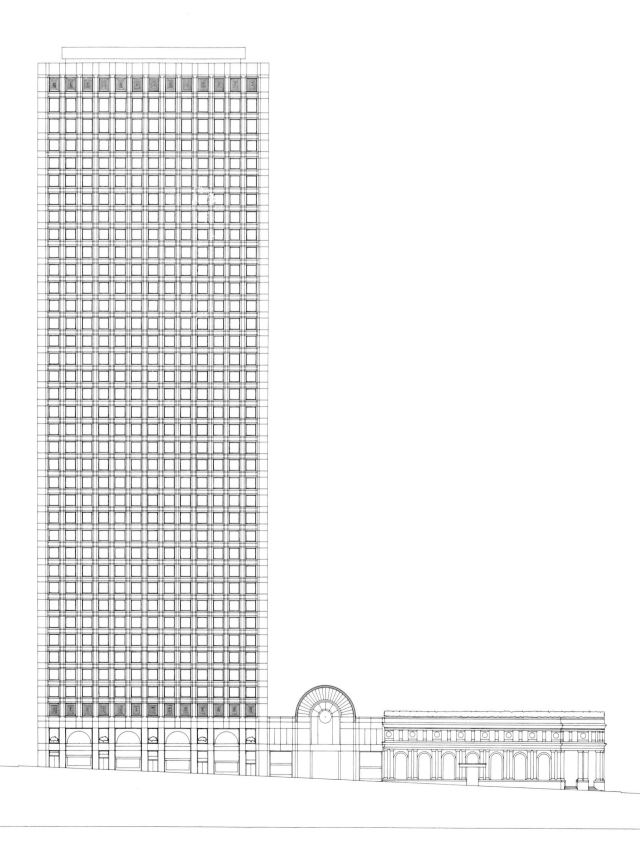

Louise M. Davies Symphony Hall
San Francisco, California

The Louise M. Davies Symphony Hall, completed in 1980, is the newest addition to the San Francisco Civic Center.

The program required a hall of approximately 1 million cubic feet to seat an audience of 3,000, along with public related foyers, lobbies and lounges, and administrative offices, rehearsal spaces, television and recording facilities, storage and other back-of-the-house requirements.

The site is a part of, but not directly in the formal geometry of, the Civic Center. It is therefore slightly relegated, dictating that the building's curved facade fall on a diagonal axis with the City Hall, and suggesting that the lobbies at each level act as glazed promenades so that the audience itself is on display and the building presents an animated and festive facade to the city streets. The design intent was to find an architectural idiom thoroughly contemporary in its expression, but consciously related in its scale and parts to the neighboring buildings, matching cornices, roof forms, colors and textures wherever possible.

The hall proper is a moderate fan shape, distributing the audience between a main orchestra level and two balcony levels. The lower balcony continues around the orchestra. Wall and ceiling surfaces are shaped for best acoustic response and consist of either painted concrete or plaster except for the wood orchestra surround at stage level. Acrylic reflector discs are suspended above the stage as required. The wall above and behind the stage is to receive a concert organ in 1983.

The structure is a composite of structural steel and reinforced concrete, depending upon the nature of the structural or acoustical need. The building is completely air conditioned. The ventilation system is designed to current best practice for sound control.

Plans (street level, orchestra level, loge level, ▷ first balcony level, second balcony level).

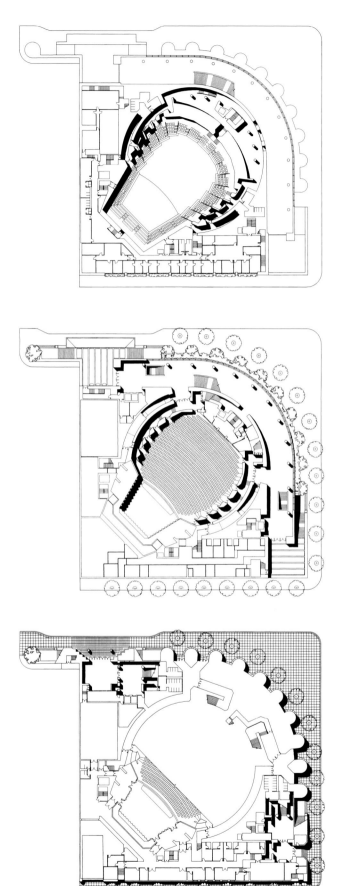
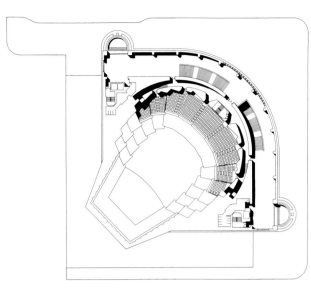
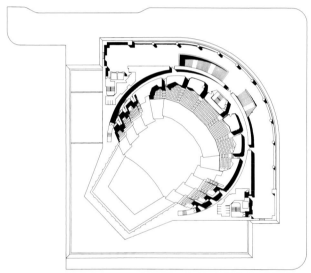

65

60'

Section. The roof and ceiling over the hall are supported by 14-foot-deep steel trusses.

A flight of exterior stairs leads to the upper ▷ foyer level at the northwest corner of the building.

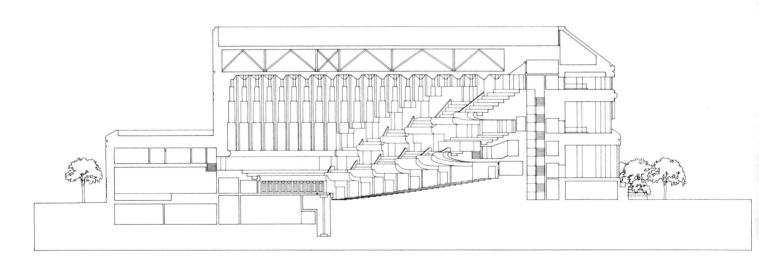

Exterior and interior view of the glazed semi-circle of the foyer, which is oriented diagonally towards the Civic Center.

Interior views of the hall. Wall and ceiling ▷ surfaces are shaped for best acoustic response, consisting of either painted concrete or plaster except for the wood orchestra surround at stage level. Acrylic reflector discs are adjusted above the stage as required.

Wells Fargo Southern California Operations Center
El Monte, California

The Wells Fargo Data Center is located in a suburban zone east of Los Angeles. The property, some 4.5 acres, was large enough to comfortably hold both the existing and new buildings. The new facility houses the check-handling, data processing and account services for Wells Fargo Bank's southern California operations as well as a cafeteria and parking for the entire complex.

By collecting the parking into a four-level structure, enough site area was saved to create a significant park, internal to the site, which is immediately accessible to occupants of both buildings. Oriented towards the park in front of the five-story data center is an entry structure with the cafeteria, serving as a central space for the people who inhabit the buildings of the complex. The sloping front facade of this element is not only a pleasant "frontispiece" for the mass of the data center but also a desired backdrop for the park. The sloping wall is sheathed in clear anodized aluminum with flush glazed vertical slots to admit light to the cafeteria. All entries to the work areas of the data center are through the generous space beneath the sloping facade which, with its lush interior landscaping, becomes an extension of the park on which it faces, and serves as a convenient meeting place for employees. Directly behind the entry structure – but for security reasons separated from it – the mechanical heart of the complex is compacted in a core stretching the entire length of the buildings. This core is stacked vertically through all five working levels and contains sophisticated mechanical and electrical equipment, allowing for the operation of the data center during normal conditions as well as during power failures.

The data center and cafeteria building is a steel moment frame structure, sheathed – with the exception of the sloping cafeteria wall – with aluminum windows and glass fiber-reinforced concrete. The window sash is extruded sheet aluminum and the entire building surface is painted in values ranging from off-white to dark brown. With relatively little glass area on any one elevation, the darker value serves to "enlarge" the windows and provide a balanced relationship of open to opaque wall area. The parking structure, constructed in a combination of precast and poured-in-place concrete, is detailed and painted to harmonize with the data center.

Site plan. The two new buildings are located in the western portion of the site.

The sloping front facade of the cafeteria struc- ▷ ture is sheathed in clear anodized aluminum with flush glazed vertical window slots.

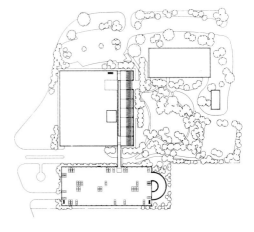

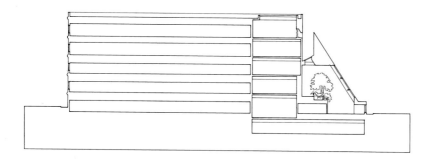

Plans (ground level, mezzanine level) and
section.

Interior view of the cafeteria which serves as a ▷
central meeting place for the employees of the
entire complex.

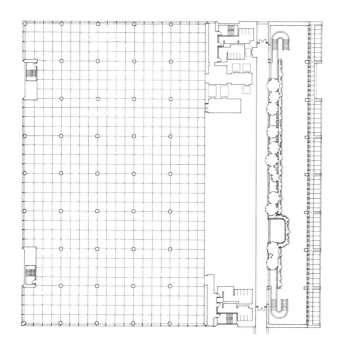

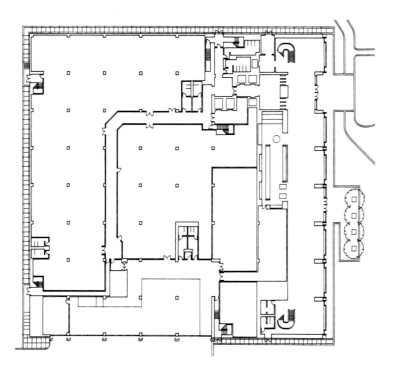

60'

Crocker Center
Los Angeles, California

The site for the Crocker Center project is situated on the highest elevation on Bunker Hill, the business and financial hub of downtown Los Angeles. Given its high visibility at a pivotal point in this part of the city, it was intended to provide a rich variety of options for people to eat, shop and be entertained.

Two office towers of 54 and 44 stories in height sit in balanced juxtaposition to one another on the east portion of the large rectangular site, while to the west a glazed pavilion is embedded in a terraced commercial structure descending the hill.

The pavilion will be enclosed in a 40-foot-high structure supporting a clear glass roof – allowing visitors views of the towers above. Constantly changing patterns of light and shadows are cast on the atrium floor. An extensive palette of cool greens, rose, copper and bronze for interior plaster surfaces, mullions, trellises, light standards and planters, as well as exterior aluminum wall panels was chosen.

Both towers are sheathed in polished red granite fitted with windows of copper-bronze insulating glass.

General view from the southeast.

Plans (ground floor, typical floor) and section. ▷

6

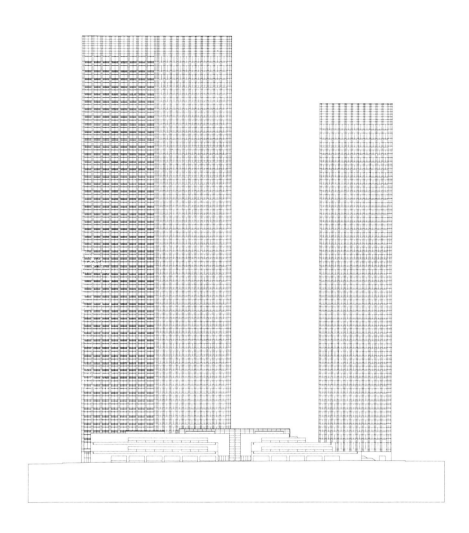

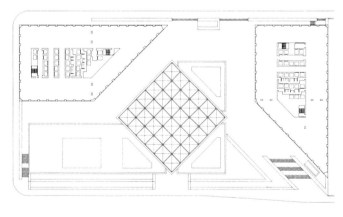

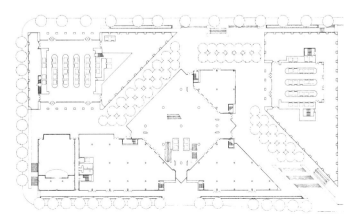

120'

Weyerhaeuser Technology Center
Tacoma, Washington

In 1971 the corporate headquarters of the Weyerhaeuser Company, one of the world's largest manufacturers of wood products, was built on a 480-acre site in suburban Tacoma. At the same time a system of roadways and paths was planned for a number of future structures on the site.

In 1974 the new building was planned to provide a close mixing of office, laboratory and development as well as support spaces in a configuration that would promote as much visual and physical contact between researchers working in different disciplines or projects as possible. Laboratories and all other work spaces were to be undedicated and anonymous, allowing for maximum functional and personnel flexibility.

The final design has three distinct but connected parts. First, a two-story glazed pavilion, the second story of which is free of exterior walls. This contains laboratory and office space. Second, a parallel link on two levels containing entry lobbies, cafeteria, meeting rooms and library. Third, a two-story space containing large-scale development equipment which is totally without exterior glazing.

The entire property was originally heavily wooded. This was partially cleared to provide a site for the corporate headquarters. The Technology Center is sited in the portion that remains wooded in a manner that as few trees as possible were cleared for the building or exterior parking. The glazing of the pavilion is clear rather than tinted or reflective glass, with the result of not changing the perception of being next to a green wall. The fact that the offices are entirely planned to be in the open makes these exterior views possible throughout the building. In addition to the open office plan, all light fixtures for general illumination are contained within the furniture pieces and no lighting is contained in the ceiling.

The structural system for the office-laboratory pavilion is a system of heavy timber girders and columns. Foundations and suspended floor slabs are of reinforced concrete. Concrete masonry shear walls brace this support structure and anchor the 220,000-square-foot plywood diaphragm roof. The development area has masonry walls which are clad with modular cedar panels.

The building seen from the south.

Site plan. The Technology Center is located ▷ north of the corporate headquarters.

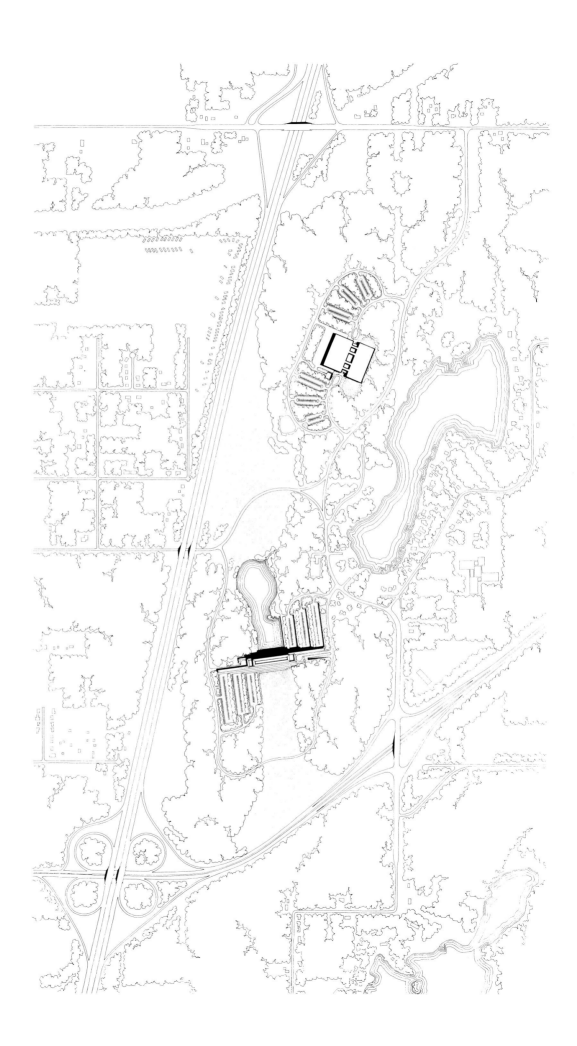

1200′

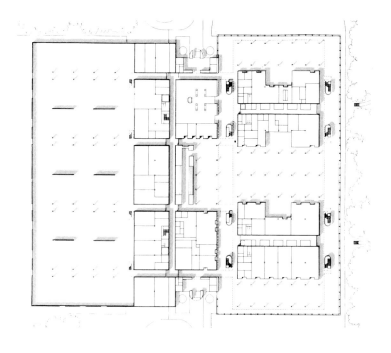

Plans (ground floor, second floor).

The Technology Center is sited in a heavily ▷ wooded portion of the site, where as few trees as possible were cleared.

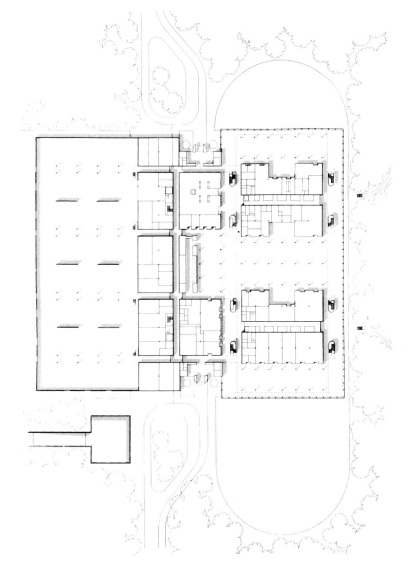

120'

View of the main entrance.

The glazing of the office pavilion is clear glass ▷
with the result of not changing the perception
of being next to a green wall.

The Portland Transit Mall
Portland, Oregon

The Portland Transit Mall extends eleven blocks along two parallel streets in the heart of downtown Portland. Completed in 1978 as the hub of a regional transit system, the mall harmoniously combines circulation systems for buses, private vehicles and pedestrians. The transit mall provides convenient transfers between bus routes and serves as a link between suburban transit stations and future light rail lines. Coordinated signals, street lights, bollards, widened sidewalks and reduced street widths establish an exclusive one-way circulation corridor which enables buses to make five stops in each direction in less than half the time previously required.

The design of the transit mall creates a lively streetscape tailored to Oregon's rainy climate. Red brick paving banded by light gray granite curbs orders the system of bus shelters, information kiosks, vendors' booths, fountains and sculptures that enrich the pedestrian experience. The broad sidewalks are landscaped with over 300 London Plane and Red Maple trees. Flowers and shrubs placed in 100 planter tubs provide additional texture and color. Refurbished light fixtures dating from the 1920's and historic cast bronze drinking fountains add a link with Portland's past.

The transit mall has 31 bronze-clad, walk-through bus shelters. At both ends of the lozenge-shaped shelter, large glass walls allow commuters to watch for buses while protected from inclement weather. The transparent overhanging roof provides additional shelter for up to 60 commuters. There are seats inside the shelter for elderly and handicapped persons. A closed-circuit television system in each bus shelter displays bus arrival and departure times. Used for the first time in the United States, the system includes back-lit maps and instructions which help the passengers use the regional transit system. Each shelter is coded by a color and a symbol keyed to seven geographic service areas. Eight trip-planning kiosks feature the closed-circuit screen, a keyboard to inquire about route numbers and bus schedules, and a free telephone linked to an information line. SOM planned and designed the transit mall in association with Lawrence Halprin and Associates.

Location plan of Portland.
1 The Portland Transit Mall.

View of a walk-through bus shelter. ▷

Pages 74–75:
The Transit Mall is a lively, colorful pedestrian environment.

2

3

5

6

The Midwest

Few architects have created landmarks that set the scale and tone of an entire city. Yet SOM/Chicago's John Hancock Center ("Big John") and Sears Tower are popularly admired for lofting Chicago's scale and skylining Chicago's vitality, even its audacity. At groundline, Chicago is punctuated with SOM's plazas and buildings: Inland Steel [2], Harris Trust, Brunswick [3], Hartford Fire Insurance, and Three First National Plaza, all in Chicago's Loop. Southwest, SOM's University of Illinois Chicago Circle Campus [4] is a crossroads of intellectual and social vitality, and eastward, towards Lake Michigan, SOM's Chicago Art Institute additions form an edge to the lakeside park. Those buildings reveal three decades of SOM's achievement, developed in powerful symbols for the Midwest's financial and cultural capital.

SOM/Chicago's strength rests upon adherence to Chicago's architectural tradition. Still the dominant expression within the modern movement, Chicago's special architecture was intimated about 1895 by John Welborn Root in his Reliance Building and Louis Sullivan in his Carson, Pirie, Scott (Schlesinger & Mayer) store. They featured slender structure, large voids, glazed transparencies, metallic arises and moulded finishes, all unified by central axes, symmetry, and tripartite facades, as in Sullivan's Prudential (Guaranty) Building in Buffalo. The Prudential, Sullivan wrote in 1896, is a tall, rational expression of the technology that carries buildings high. That ideal suffered from Root's early death and Sullivan's eclipse, but when in 1981 he stated SOM/Chicago's goal, the late SOM/Chicago partner Fazlur Khan reaffirmed that ideal: "the visible expression of technology in architecture."

Chicago itself has only recently cherished its heritage. Although Buffalo gained Sullivan's Prudential, St. Louis his Wainwright and Owatonna his National Bank, Chicago ignored Sullivan for major commissions. Even his most celebrated disciple, the incomparably fecund Frank Lloyd Wright, did not design Chicago's important commercial or civic buildings. Instead, Chicago often sought Roman and Gothic designers, and their Wrigley and Chicago Tribune Buildings of about 1925 resemble the Gothic scenery the philanthropist John D. Rockefeller gave to the University of Chicago, despite Thorstein Veblen's championship of a functional alternative. That architecture

1 Skyline of Chicago, Illinois.
2 Inland Steel Building, Chicago, Illinois.
3 Brunswick Building, Chicago, Illinois.
4 University of Illinois, Chicago Circle Campus, Chicago, Illinois.
5 Art Institute of Chicago, Chicago, Illinois.
6 Oak Ridge, Tennessee.
7 Lake Meadows Housing, Chicago, Illinois.

7

8

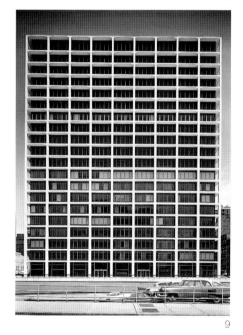

9

might spring from program, technology and native culture, as Sullivan urged, was a dream which, save Wright, nearly died with Sullivan in 1924.

How ironic therefore to find Sullivan's great Stock Exchange Hall preserved inside SOM's new buildings for the Chicago Art Institute [5]! There, at Chicago's center of the arts, Sullivan's Trading Room has been moved and lovingly conserved with SOM's help, and the Exchange's arched entrance is now a freestanding sculpture in SOM's gardens. In the years between the classical Art Institute and SOM's new additions lies a story of Chicago's growing pride, which was encouraged by a succession of SOM partners, including Hartmann, Graham and Netsch who won the confidence of Chicago's civic leaders.

What Chicago's leaders wanted was strong imagery announcing corporate and cultural presence in urban settings. Fortunately (and the fortune lay in his declining to go to Harvard a year earlier), Ludwig Mies van der Rohe was attracted to Chicago. Heralded by his elegant German Pavilion at Barcelona and Tugendhat House at Brno, Czechoslovakia, Mies slowly won commissions. Meanwhile, his intellectual discipline in synopsis, generalization and symbol compelled a following. Arriving in Chicago fresh from study at the University of Pennsylvania, Bruce Graham joined SOM's office in 1949, and, like many designers, found in Mies a master to admire.

When Graham joined its Chicago office, SOM already enjoyed respect for its wartime training centers on Chicago's piers and Oak Ridge Laboratories [6] where SOM designers Walter Netsch and Myron Goldsmith had won their partnerships. In the 1950's, SOM completed the Lake Meadows Housing [7], started the Air Force Academy, began major projects for the State Universities of Iowa and Illinois, erected the office buildings for Harris Trust and Inland Steel, and finished the extraordinary Kitt Peak National Observatory in Arizona. The observatory was designed by Goldsmith whose fidelity to refined structural shapes is visible in his printing plant for "The Republic" in Columbus, Indiana, built in the 1960's. Visibly different were the arresting forms Netsch composed for UICC and the Air Force Academy. And still different was the work of the rising designer, Graham, who was elected partner in 1960, after completing Inland Steel and Harris Trust. The diversity among SOM/Chicago's designers was greater than any differences among

10

11

12

8 Harris Trust and Savings Bank, Chicago, Illinois.
9 Hartford Fire Insurance Building, Chicago, Illinois.
10 John Hancock Center, Chicago, Illinois.
11 Sears Tower, Chicago, Illinois.
12 Headquarters of Baxter Travenol, Deerfield, Illinois.

13

14

15

their geometries or structural expressions. Each artistically creative and intellectually avid, the three enjoyed different types of client and perceptions of architecture. Graham led the colossal office building projects for John Hancock and Sears, while Netsch made award-winning university buildings and sought to relate SOM to liberal causes. Goldsmith was fascinated by esoteric technical problems, like the Kitt Peak Observatory, where technical precision was paramount.

The Air Force Academy at Colorado Springs (designed 1954–57; built 1956–62) proved SOM's aesthetic talent, technical skill and project organization. In the 1950's and 1960's, no other architectural firm could have carried so vast a project to such depth of concept, quality, and refinement or speed in completion. Nearly thirty years ago (1957), the Inland Steel Building showed Chicago the promise of modern urban form. Shortly, Harris Trust [8] juxtaposed its two-story plenum and open steel frame against its classical masonry neighbor. Then came the Hartford Fire Insurance Building [9], where structural realism demanded the tapered columns, thin floor slabs and inflected connections. For the John Hancock Building [10], structural logic was carried to a breathtakingly tall structure rising from only a fraction of its site, and the exposed diagonals were tied into the steel exoskeleton at strategic intersections. The epitome was the Sears Tower [11], 1,470 feet tall, enclosing a gigantic 4.4 million square feet, all carried by perimetal tubes, which determined architectural form, as designers Graham and Khan intended.

SOM's structurally based emblems appear often throughout the Midwest. Some are literal, like the cables and suspended roof of Baxter Travenol [12]. In Des Moines, Iowa, a view of the American Republic Insurance Headquarters [13] dramatizes four pairs of steel hinges. In contrast to literalism, structural expression is sometimes abstract, as beside the freeway in Kansas City, Missouri, where the Business Men's Assurance Headquarters [14] brings welded steel piers and spandrels to one vertical surface without differentiation throughout the 19-story tower. In the 1970's, SOM/Chicago, like SOM/San Francisco, often subordinated structural expression. The allusive form sometimes hid structure until revealed by interior illumination, as in the Industrial Trust Building in Muncie, Indiana [15], and the Fourth Financial Bank in Wichita, Kansas [16]. Neither structural nor functional expression was so

16

17

13 American Republic Insurance Headquarters, Des Moines, Iowa.
14 Business Men's Assurance Headquarters, Kansas City, Missouri.
15 Industrial Trust & Savings Bank, Muncie, Indiana.
16 Fourth Financial Center, Wichita, Kansas.
17 Columbus City Hall, Columbus, Indiana.
18 One Magnificent Mile, Chicago, Illinois.

18

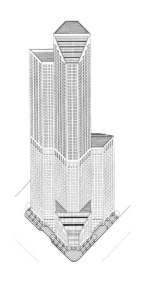

19

20

21

compelling as the formal envelope for SOM/ Chicago's Centennial Center at Schaumburg, Illinois. At the City Hall in Columbus, Indiana [17], designed by SOM/San Francisco, two long cantilevers, clad in brick masonry, subordinate structure to emblematic intent. Still, the dominant expression in SOM's Midwestern work remained technological. The vibrant massing of Chicago's One Magnificent Mile [18] and the articulated fenestration in Chicago's Olympia Centre [19] originate in the versatility of tube structural systems. Chicago's 33 West Monroe Street [20], a compact 28-story building, reduces exposed surfaces and mechanical core, clads its compact mass with deep spandrels and thermal glass, and wraps its offices around three multistory atria.

SOM/Chicago has never been monolithic. The transitional nodes and sequential spaces in the Caterpillar Tractor Training Center model [21] reflect earlier articulated form in Netsch's Air Force Academy Chapel and UICC buildings for Behavioral Sciences [22] and Architecture of the early 1960's. Intent upon defining spaces by angled walls and roofs, Netsch aimed at solving three problems simultaneously: identity of structural points, integration of mechanical equipment, and creation of spaces formed by integrating wall, roof and floor. Basing his initial planning on superimposed rotated squares, Netsch selected mass or void from the diagonals, points and hexagons within a lattice or field. After computer graphics assisted his three-dimensional study, Netsch's selection was a plastic choice, and his Lindquist Center at the University of Iowa [23] and Art Museum for Miami University at Oxford, Ohio, justify his hard-won study.

An increasing concern for building's context is evident in SOM's Midwestern work in the 1970's. For the Menninger Foundation in Topeka, Kansas [24], SOM/Chicago partner James DeStefano, starting with clustered bedrooms, cottages and courtyards, achieved a scale compatible with existing buildings. Both the Pillsbury Center and St. Paul Town Square towers [25] accommodate transit ways, enclose pedestrian circulation, and sustain significant vistas. Muncie's Industrial Trust & Savings Bank respects existing cornice lines, and Columbus' City Hall directs its plaza and forecourt towards historic Main Street and the County Courthouse. A similar care for context explains the faceted profile of the First Wisconsin Bank in Madison [26], Minneapolis' Lutheran Brotherhood [27], One Magnificent

22

23

24

19 Olympia Centre, Chicago, Illinois.
20 33 West Monroe Street, Chicago, Illinois.
21 Caterpillar Training Center, Peoria, Illinois.
22 Behavioral Sciences Building, University of Illinois, Chicago Circle Campus, Chicago, Illinois.
23 Lindquist Center, University of Iowa, Iowa City, Iowa.
24 The Menninger Foundation, Topeka, Kansas.

25

26

27
28

Mile in Chicago, and Three First National Plaza [28], also in Chicago. Massing its tallest tower on Chicago Avenue, the Olympia Centre presents only its lower elements to Michigan Avenue. Added to those formal contextual responses were the urban amenities gained by having enclosed plazas, atria and lobbies. The lobby at Three First National Plaza is a multilevel interchange, and the eight-story atrium at Pillsbury Center, which traverses a second-level skyway, contains shops and restaurants, while the concourse at Town Square in St. Paul offers fountains, pools, and waterfalls among restaurants and stores disposed on three levels, all related to a major department store. Residential, retail and office space are combined in One Magnificent Mile and also in the Olympia Centre, where a department store surrounds a skylighted atrium.

In 1971, SOM/Chicago conducted a two-year study of 7,000 acres in the center of Chicago. Guided by SOM/Chicago partner Roger Seitz, the Chicago 21 Plan [29] evolved a New Town, proposed to be a total environment south of the central business district, recreational parks on the Lake front, apartments on the Chicago River shoreline, and a transitway along a State Street shopping corridor. Started in 1977, 40-acre Dearborn Park [30] will offer 3,000 housing units in parklike settings. The Chicago 21 Plan reflects the talent that has won SOM/Chicago the confidence of Chicago's civic and cultural leaders, who in 1982 awarded SOM/Chicago responsibility for planning the Chicago World's Fair [31] scheduled for 1992 – a great opportunity to evolve enduring urban functions and symbols for Chicago and the Midwest.

25 St. Paul Town Square, St. Paul, Minnesota.
26 First Wisconsin Plaza, Madison, Wisconsin.
27 Lutheran Brotherhood Building, Minneapolis, Minnesota.
28 Three First National Plaza, Chicago, Illinois.
29 Chicago 21 Plan.
30 Dearborn Park, Chicago, Illinois.
31 Chicago World's Fair 1992.

29

30
31

33 West Monroe Street
Chicago, Illinois

The primary goal in designing the 33 West Monroe building was to create an energy-efficient investment office building for a developer's budget at the time of an unpredictable leasing period in Chicago. The solution was to optimize all building systems, including the substructure, superstructure, HVAC, exterior and vertical transportation. The savings thus achieved permitted the designers to add tenant amenities that would create a marketable, institutional quality building.

During the conceptual design phase, two building configurations were developed. The first was a traditional 1,000,000-square-foot, slender 45-story building with small floors. This design was compared with the atrium building design which was a 28-story building occupying the entire site and containing a total of 1,000,000 square feet with office floors ranging from 30,050 square feet to 37,400 square feet. The atrium design optimized all the necessary building systems, making both the construction cost and operating costs more economical than the first design.

The final solution for 33 West Monroe was to vertically stack three atria formed by overhanging office floors rising 7 to 12 stories. The atria serve as lobbies for the floors that rise above. Glass-enclosed office floors overlook each atrium, illuminated by natural light from the exterior window wall. The atrium concept provides greater perimeter glass for each floor, a stronger leasing concept and a tremendous mechanical advantage. An energy-efficient exterior envelope using dual glazed, semi-reflective glass reduces heat gain, minimizes heat loss and affords a comfortable work environment.

The building's relationship to surrounding buildings is reinforced by the choice of exterior paint color which harmonizes with the stainless steel Inland Steel Building directly across the street to the north. The 28-story 33 West Monroe Building further respects the neighboring 19-story Inland Steel Building in its massing which begins to step back from the street at the 19th floor. Its orientation along the edge of the side visually anchors the building to the corner, reinforcing the open space of the First National Bank Plaza across the street.

Designed in the tradition of the Chicago School, the building is a pure expression of the simple structural frame.

Section.

View of the building from First National Bank ▷ Plaza. The 28-story building respects the neighboring 19-story Inland Steel Building in its massing which begins to step back at the 19th floor.

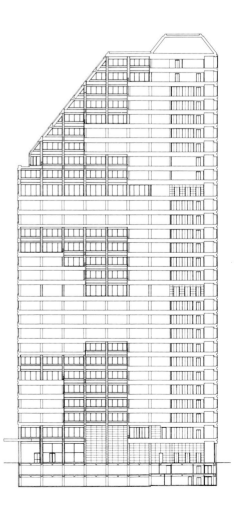

Plans (ground floor, typical donut floor, typical
U floor, typical full floor).

30'

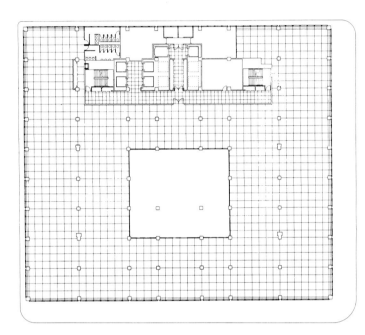

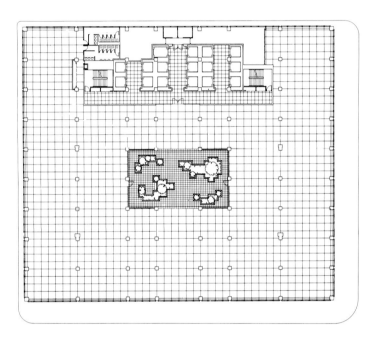

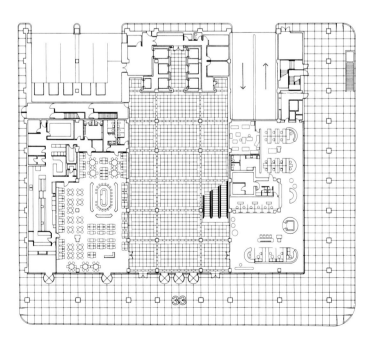

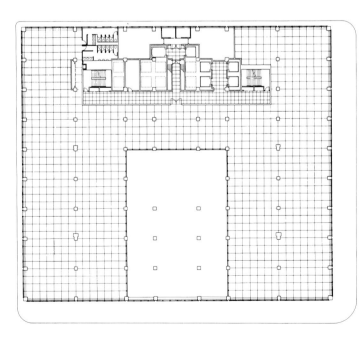

The building is a pure expression of the simple
structural frame.

Three First National Plaza
Chicago, Illinois

Completed early in 1982, the Three First National Plaza complex occupies a prime partial-block location near the financial center and downtown commercial district of Chicago's Loop. The project comprises a 57-story tower, an 11-story element which engages an existing private club, and a central nine-story glazed public lobby.

The configuration of the new tower was designed to retain a degree of openness along busy Madison Avenue and to minimize the disruption of views from the neighboring 60-story First National Bank Building. The sawtooth geometry, which provides multiple corner offices, makes a transition on the top six levels to stepped greenhouse offices with views over the city toward Lake Michigan. Just as the massing of Three First National Plaza is designed to relate to its neighbor tower, the carnelian granite cladding reinforces their complementary relationship. A second level walkway further links the two structures.

Bay windows, a traditional element of Chicago turn-of-the-century architecture, are a central feature of the tower, designed to provide light and views for prestige tenants. Projecting from the structural tube, the bays emphasize the tower's vertical expression. Cantilevered from the concrete and steel structural system, the bronze reflective glass bays are framed in warm gray aluminum spandrels which act as louvers for the decentralized mechanical system.

On three sides, office areas and mezzanine balconies look onto the central nine-story public space. A stepped steel truss structure, repeating the sawtooth geometry on a horizontal plane, supports the clear glass enclosure. Connected below grade both to Chicago's rapid transit system and underground commercial arcade network, the lobby is designed as an indoor plaza in the Chicago tradition of open public spaces. A Henry Moore sculpture will enhance the plaza, which is designed to add street-level animation with its granite paving, bronze detailing, landscaping and specialty shopping area.

The sawtooth geometry of the building provides multiple corner offices.

In its stairstepped shape the steel truss ▷ structure of the atrium repeats the sawtooth configuration of the enclosing building walls.

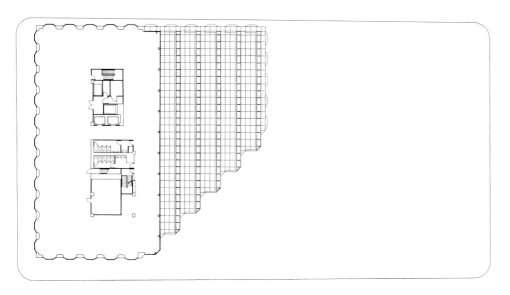

Plans (ground plan, typical floor, upper floor).

Axonometric view of the upper portion of ▷ the tower.

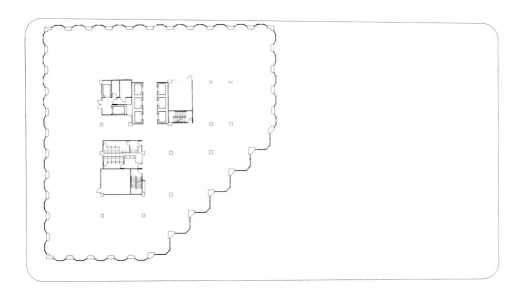

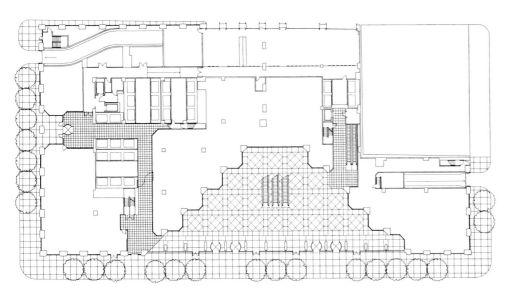

30′

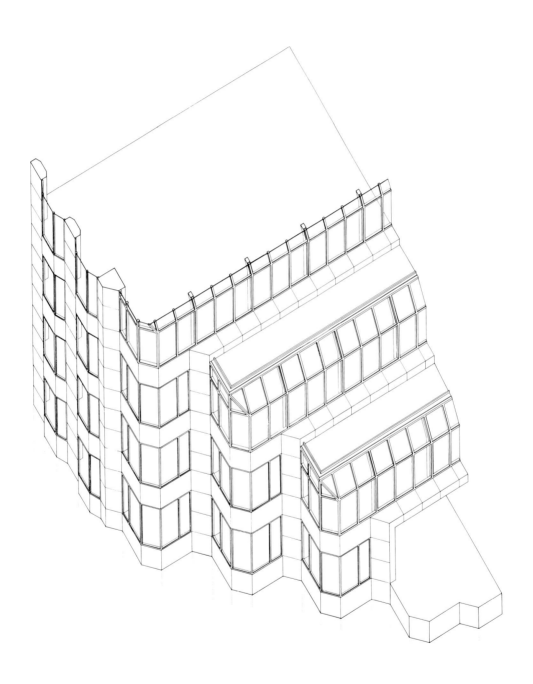

One Magnificent Mile
Chicago, Illinois

One Magnificent Mile, to be completed in 1983, is situated at the northern end of one of the most elegant and prestigious shopping avenues in the nation. The multi-use tower will contain commercial space on the first three levels, office space on floors 4 to 19, and 181 luxury condominiums at the top of the building.

The building floor plans and profile were developed as an expression of both the problems and opportunities of the small, angular lot at the corner of Oak Street and Michigan Avenue, and of the logic and structural possibilities of the bundled-tube system. Three hexagonal concrete tubes with punched window openings rise 57, 49 and 21 stories and are joined together to resist wind loads as a bundled tube. The top of the 21-story element bears a two-story mechanical floor, which, as it is carried across the entire tower floor area, sharply divides the office levels from the residential floors by a broad horizontal line. Following interior functions, the fenestration is treated in different manners below and above this visual division.

The tubes' geometric shapes and varying heights result from extensive studies of desirable views from the high-rise condominiums and of the potential shadow cast over the nearby Oak Street park and beach. Computer simulation determined the optimum height at which no shadow would blight these recreation areas. In addition, the faceted shape skillfully avoids the impression that the new building turns its back on any of its significant neighbors, relating well to adjacent structures, to Lake Shore Drive and to the high-rise buildings on Michigan Avenue.

The 57-story tower element in the middle of the bundle is topped by a glazed roof, sloping towards the northeast, with a view of the beach and the lake, and covering greenhouses and recreation facilities for tenants' use. Reflecting this scheme, a five-story hexagonal entrance pavilion in front of this high tower element also has a glazed roof sloping northeast towards the corner of Michigan Avenue and Oak Street.

The tower will be clad in granite with clear windows at the commercial level, gray reflective glass for the offices and gray tinted glass for the condominiums.

View of One Magnificent Mile from the south ▷
with North Michigan Avenue in the foreground.

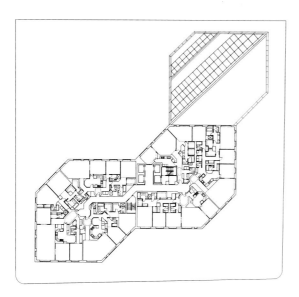

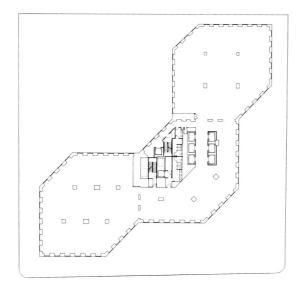

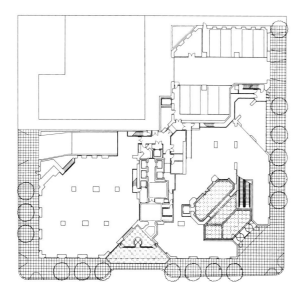

Plans (ground level, typical office floor, typical condominium floor)

Axonometric view of the building. ▷

30'

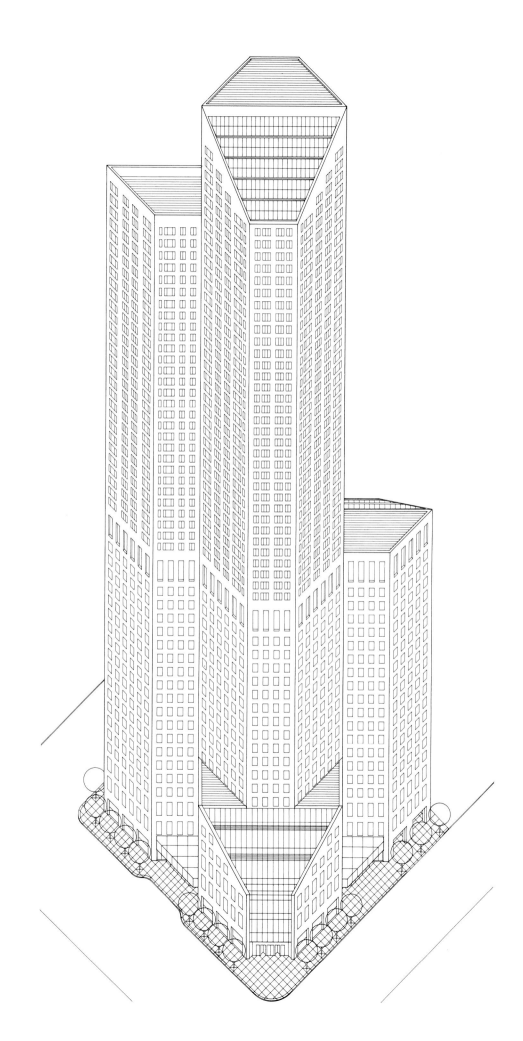

Reorganization and Expansion of the Art Institute of Chicago
Chicago, Illinois

In 1970, the Art Institute of Chicago commissioned SOM to develop a comprehensive master plan for the reorganization and physical expansion of the museum and its art school. The plan comprised a long-range project for new space to the east at Columbus Drive and on air rights over the railroad tracks to the north and south, and a specific phased construction program.

New construction in the first phase provided a circulation spine toward the ultimate East Entrance and additional gallery areas by adding a second level above the galleries around McKinlock Court. To reduce the apparent scale of the addition yet accommodate large 20th century works, a sloping roof was designed. Window openings respect the rhythm and character of the original court designed by Coolidge and Hodgson in 1924.

Major elements of the 1977 Columbus Drive additions are the School of Art, an auditorium, the Chicago Architecture Gallery, a members' lounge overlooking Lake Michigan and two public restaurants.

The 110,000-square-foot School of Art addition was designed to accommodate 1,000 full-time students as well as student enrichment programs and adult education. A school gallery integrates the addition into the museum while providing independent access and security. The simple form and detailing of the addition result from the physical and visual context of the lakefront Grant Park and are an extension of the materials of the original buildings.

The low, central element at Columbus Drive houses the Chicago Architecture Gallery. On axis with the three-story main building, the reverse pediment of the East Additions allows the original museum to be seen from Grant Park and Lake Shore Drive. Limestone cladding, slim mirror glass windows and sloped metal roofs were designed to complement the earlier structures and make the additions a restrained contemporary foreground to the 1892 main building.

The Chicago Architecture Gallery now incorporates the restored Adler and Sullivan Stock Exchange Trading Room. Working with Vinci & Kenny, architects for the reconstruction, SOM designed the building shell with skylights to illuminate the original clerestories of the 1893 Trading Room.

General view of the Art Institute with the
new additions in the foreground.

The entrance to the new wing is oriented on a
diagonal and overlooks Columbus Gardens.

Overall plan and elevation. ▷

120'

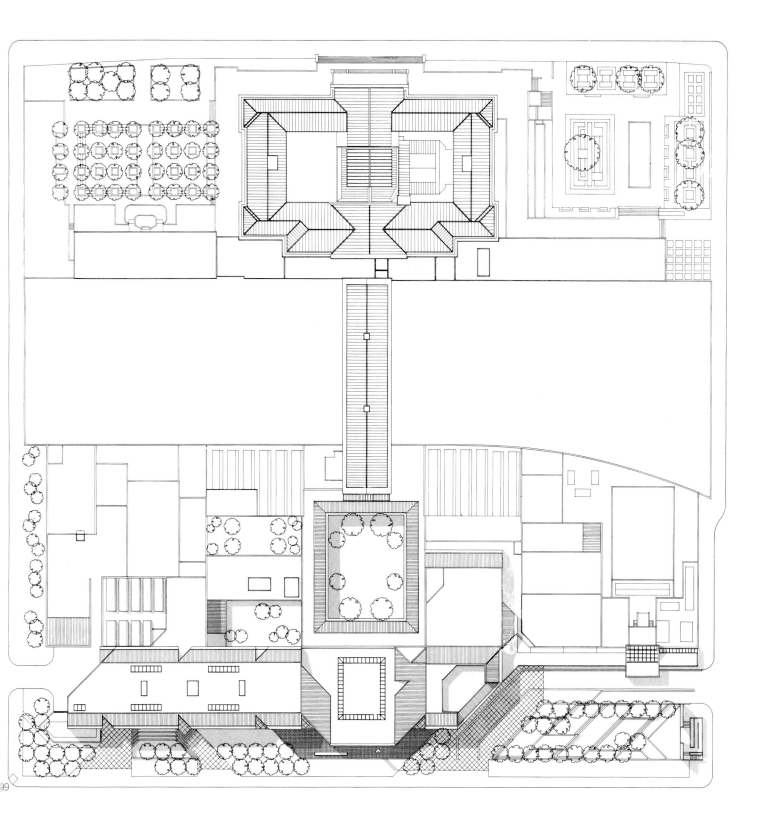

The Sullivan arch, saved from the demolished Stock Exchange Building, forms the gateway to the eastern portion of the museum.

A glazed facade acts as a backdrop for Isamu Noguchi's sculpture "Celebration of the 200th Anniversary of the Founding of the Republic," which is enhanced by an ornamental reflecting pool.

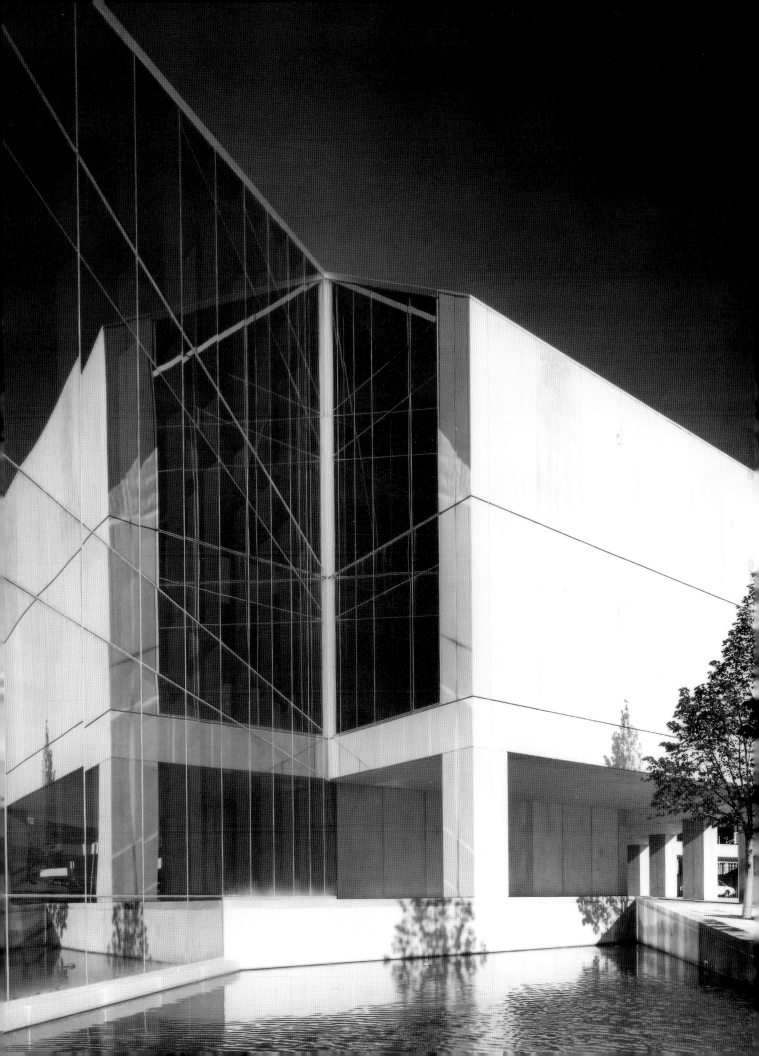

Headquarters of Baxter Travenol, Inc.
Deerfield, Illinois

Completed in 1975 on a rolling, 179-acre site northwest of Chicago, the corporate head-quarters for Baxter Travenol, Inc. was designed to accommodate the pharmaceutical company's continuous reorganization and expansion. The master plan concept consists of a flexible cluster of modular office pavilions expanding north and south from a central facilities building and parking garages. Linked by an underground pedestrian network and by corner second-level bridges, the long-span steel structures function as autono-mous modules or larger shared spaces. Future expansion can be achieved by additional modules followed by a new, similarly flexible cluster.
Within the campus plan, two double-helix garages are centrally located to minimize walking distances and eliminate open-air car parks. All four stories of the stepped steel structure's are bordered with planter boxes concealing automobiles from view.
The central facilities building, which houses an auditorium and training center on the bermed lower level, features a 1,000-seat cafeteria on the 24-foot-high main level. A stayed-cable suspended roof is supported by two steel pylons rising 35 feet above its metal deck. Visible from an adjacent expressway, the twin masts give an easily recog-nized identity to the complex.
Four office pavilions and a low executive building complete the original campus. These two- and three-story modules each have a dominant interior color scheme for easy orientation. Closed offices are placed along the short elevations so that open-plan work stations benefit from the maximum light and views over the site. In the executive pavilion, perimeter suites surround central conference and board rooms.
The crisp exterior cladding of off-white painted metal and infill panels of full-height, semi-reflective dual glazing in stainless steel mullions reflect the client's precise, clean image.
Landscaping, more formal near the buildings and roadways, re-creates natural Midwest prairie conditions over most of the site. Man-made ponds provide drainage, storm water retention and flood control.

Section of the central facilities building.

Site plan. ▷

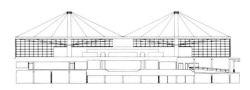

Plan of the central facilities building (main level).

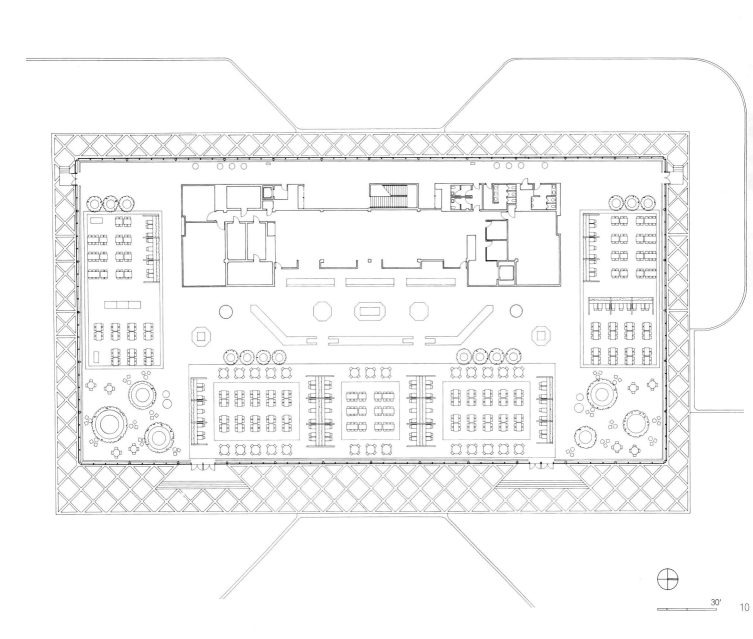

30'

The 1,000-seat cafeteria accommodating the
entire staff at one sitting offers a variety of
seating possibilities along the glass-walled
perimeter.

Pages 106–107:
The dramatic cable-suspended roof structure
of the central facilities building gives an easily
recognizable identity to the complex.

First Wisconsin Center
Milwaukee, Wisconsin

The corporate headquarters for the largest bank in Wisconsin was completed in down-town Milwaukee in 1974 on a six-acre site composed of three city blocks. There is a substantial slope from north to south and the southern portion of the site is bisected by a major roadway. The character of the development was significantly influenced by these site conditions as well as the owner's previously announced plans to build a 40-story tower.

The solution for the design problem of creating two distinctive images for the banking facility and announced office tower was to set a 40-story tower toward the center of the site above a double-level glass-enclosed podium. This low-rise structure respects the scale of existing buildings while softening the transition between the horizontal street and vertical tower. On the first level of the banking facility are the main banking hall, safe-deposit area and a landscaped garden. This feeling of openness within a weather-protected parklike space is continued on the second level by a skylit galleria which contains the commercial lending divisions, shops, restaurants and clubs.

The galleria bridges the street to a separate 850-car garage on the southern segment of the site. The truss bridge provides a sheltered pedestrian path through the superblock and is the first element in a potential expansion of an elevated covered walkway system.

The white-coated aluminum tower provides smaller floor areas for the corporate and rental offices. Although a 40-foot structural grid was established for the site, the efficiency of the tower structure required a reduced perimeter column spacing of 20 feet. The transfer of this structure back to the larger podium grid is achieved through V-shaped transfer beams expressed as a distinctive exterior design element. The structural system for the steel tower is based on the framed tube concept combined with belt trusses.

Plan (typical office floor).

General view of the complex. ▷

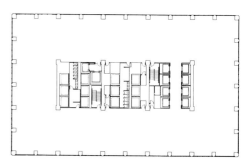

Plan (ground level).

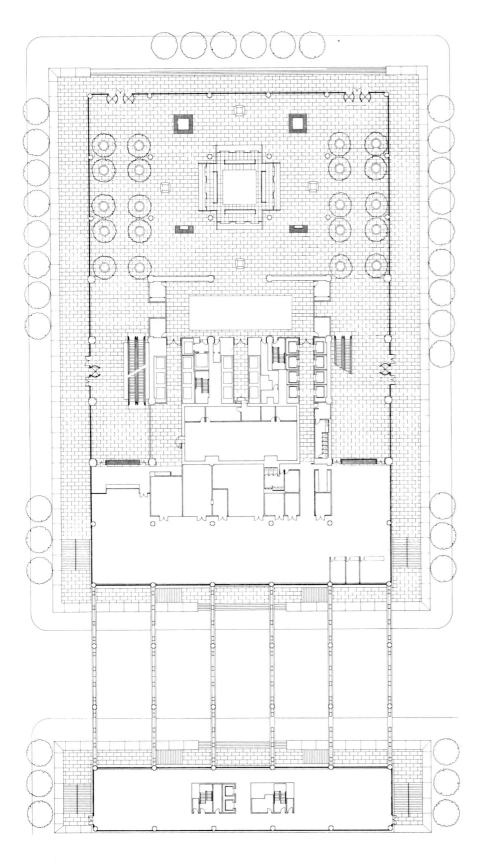

30'

1"

View of the banking hall situated on the ground level.

View of the two-story skylit atrium. Mezzanine floors along the side bays form a visual enclosure for the parklike interior.

Pages 112–113:
The structural system for the steel tower is based on the framed tube concept combined with belt trusses.

First Wisconsin Plaza
Madison, Wisconsin

This nine-story bank and office building was completed in 1974 on a site in downtown Madison. In an area designated for redevelopment, the building directly faces the State Capitol across Capitol Square, a parkland mall. The 500,000-square-foot building includes 140,000 square feet of banking space, 175,000 square feet of tenant offices, a commercial mall, a restaurant and health club, and 130,000 square feet of parking space.

The northeastern exposure of the building faces the street with a straight nine-story wall of glass, while the exposure facing Capitol Square is staggered down with sloping glass roofs to first floor height. Offices on the upper floors wrap around a fourth floor roof garden on three sides, gaining an attractive view of the Capitol Square in the southwest. This treatment of the building adds scale and compatibility with the picturesque architecture of the 19th century Capitol.

Rather than an open plaza, the Wisconsin climate dictated an open, airy internal environment sheathed in glass. The Bauhaus-style curtain wall eliminated typical spandrel panels while providing an economical solution for the building's skin of white painted aluminum mullions and double glazed glass in 3-foot by 5-foot panels. The mechanical system is expressed as a design element of the curtain wall. A series of air risers and induction units painted blue and water risers painted yellow is exposed and set behind an outer grid of white mullions. On the main banking floor, five murals designed by the artist Valerio Adami integrate the open spaces with the bright color scheme of the rest of the interiors. Three-story greenhouses expand from the structural bays, creating internal garden spaces.

This was one of the first adaptations in an office building of the atrium concept, which has since gained considerable importance in the United States. The energy-efficient design allows the curtain wall to capture sunlight, yet the heating load and ratio of glass to square footage are very efficient in spite of full glazing.

Southwest elevation.

Plan (ground floor) and section. ▷

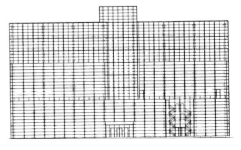

1

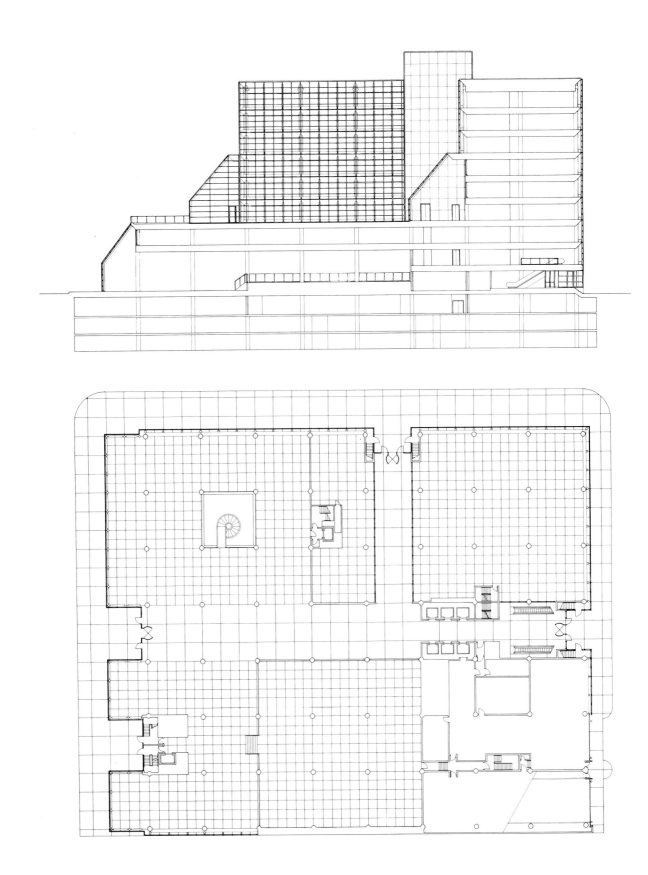

30'

Three-story greenhouses expand from the structural bays, creating internal garden spaces.

Pages 118–119:
An open, airy environment sheathed in glass was chosen in response to Wisconsin's harsh climate.

FIRST WISCONSIN PLAZA

Pillsbury Center
Minneapolis, Minnesota

The design of the Pillsbury Center 1,900,000-square-foot investment office complex on a full block in the city center had to integrate the requirements of two primary tenants, a highly structured urban site and one of the most stringent energy codes in the United States. Two identically shaped towers of 40 and 22 stories, stepping down in two-floor increments at the eight lower levels, were designed to give distinct identities and discrete, flexible facilities to the Pillsbury Company and the First National Bank of Minneapolis. The towers were sited on a strong diagonal axis, allowing separate landscaped plazas which further distinguish the dual occupancies. Both height and massing were also a direct response to the urban context. Along the diagonal axis, views of the historic city hall are preserved at the pedestrian level and from the neighboring 51-story IDS Center to the southwest.

A key design intent was to establish the complex as a major focal node in the city's extensive skyway system. Linking the two towers, a stepped eight-story atrium lobby with multi-faceted triangular panels of clear glazing accommodates second-level pedestrian bridges to surrounding buildings to the north and west and also allows an additional link to the east. Inserted along the narrow diagonal axis, the atrium is carved into the towers' stepped elements to form opposing geometries beneath column transfer trusses. With shops and restaurants on two levels, the atrium is designed to become a spacious indoor plaza and year-round activity center for the city. Paved in dark carnelian granite and accented by stainless steel finishes, the bright, column-free space is highlighted by a suspended Loren Madsen gravity sculpture.

Light travertine and gray-tinted glass, set off above dark carnelian plinth and plazas, were chosen to complement and illuminate the physical forms within the context of the surrounding urban environment. Heavy insulation applied to the concrete structural frames and dual glazing attenuate heat loss and solar gain while extensive use of outside air for cooling reduces energy consumption. The city's first major office complex to be designed in compliance with the Minnesota Energy Code, Pillsbury Center employs a heat pump system and central supply from the city's underground steam distribution network.

General view of the complex.

View of the atrium from the mezzanine level. ▷

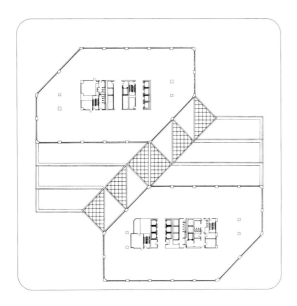

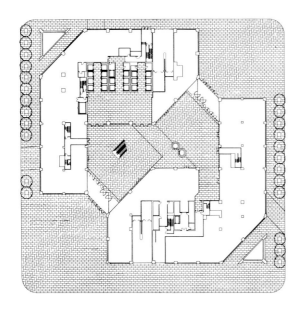

Plans (ground level, second floor, typical floor).

Elevation of the 40-story tower with section ▷ through the atrium.

60'

St. Paul Town Square
St. Paul, Minnesota

Town Square, completed in 1980, is a prime example of an economically viable combination of office, retail, and commercial spaces integrated with recreational and civic-
oriented uses to draw people to the city's core. It includes a large, two-block retail podium
containing retail shops and restaurants and a major department store; office towers of
25 and 27 stories; a 16-story, 250-room hotel; underground parking for 500 vehicles; and
an enclosed city-owned park.
Town Square is the focal point of three urban transitways in St. Paul: pedestrian circulation along 7th Street; the extensive downtown skyway system; and a planned people
mover system connecting the large populations of the capital area and near suburbs
with the downtown core. Siting of the various elements of the project respond directly
to these factors. The juxtaposed towers are chiseled in plan allowing the people mover
system to pass between them, while circulation and structure are likewise designed to
accommodate the future station at the podium's roof level.
The podium is kept at two levels to relate to the scale of neighboring buildings. A strong
theme of rounded columns and curved spandrels is used on the exterior and interior
shopping areas. These rounded forms, extended to the cladding of the office towers,
provide sculptured facades that continually change with the movement of the sun.
A 2.5-acre public park under the glazed atrium further emphasizes Town Square's role as
a focal point of the downtown core. Over 300 species of plants can be found throughout
the greenhouse area. The protected oasis includes an amphitheater, a children's play area,
lecture and display areas, and is also suitable for concerts, parties and cultural events.
Visual unity and spaciousness for all levels is provided by abundant greenery, extensive
skylights, large openings between levels, and a fountain which visually flows from the
park level down to the concourse level.
Well water from St. Paul's aquifer, with a constant temperature of 55 degrees, is used
in heat pumps to heat and cool the complex, lowering energy consumption to approximately half that used by conventional high-rise buildings.

General view of the complex (model).

On top of a large retail podium featuring an ▷
enclosed town square environment, two office
towers and a hotel are located.

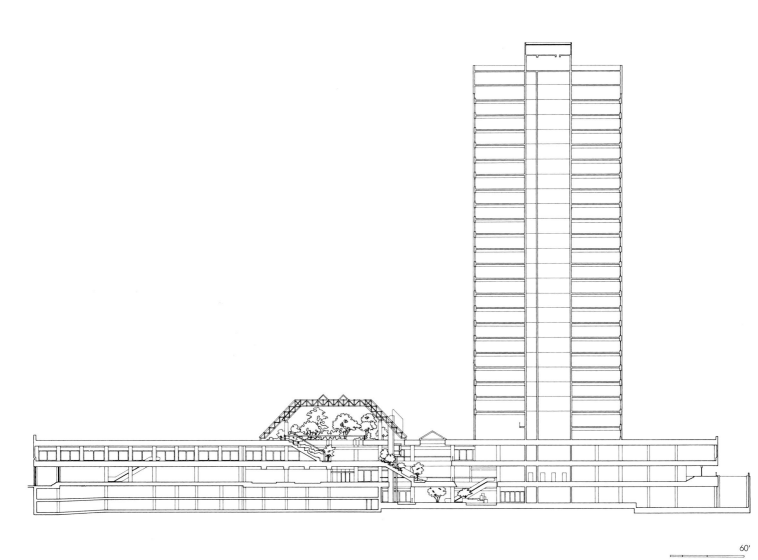

60'

Section through one of the office towers and
the atrium.

View into the public park under the glazed
atrium.

Lutheran Brotherhood Building
Minneapolis, Minnesota

The shape of the Lutheran Brotherhood Building is the result of urban context and owner's requirements. The site, which is flat and uneventful, is centrally placed and has a number of important neighbors, especially the monumental Hennepin County Government Center immediately across the street. Studies indicated that the best relationship to the Government Center was obtained when the mass of the new building became horizontal rather than vertical, and that the small park across the street was framed most successfully when the building's length extended the full block.

Two programmatic factors strongly influenced the building's form. The first was the large variation in the size and nature of the spaces required – ranging from typical floors of individual offices to those of open landscape, data processing and computers. In addition, the client's important place in the cultural as well as business life of the community demanded more public space than customary, including areas for assembly and exhibition, a library, appropriate customer and building services, and a large and flexible dining facility.

The design responds through a long 17-story rectangle whose main facade steps up in a series of three tilted and stepped planes. The lowest typical office floor is considerably less than the public floors at the street and skyway levels, but more than twice the area of the uppermost floor. The building's vertical services are distributed along the vertical plane of the northeast facade to assure the flexibility of the office floors and to leave the public spaces below unencumbered.

The major part of the dining facility is expressed as a glazed, barrel-vaulted room extending out from the building mass and overlooking the park. The building's exterior wall is a flush skin of brightly reflective and energy-efficient copper tinted glass, set in dark red enamelled aluminum frames. The street level is a rusticated pink granite from Texas.

Section.

The main facade rises in a series of three ▷ tilted and stepped planes.

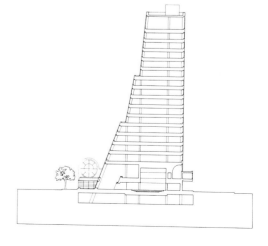

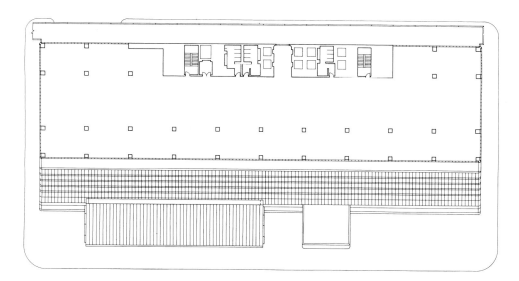

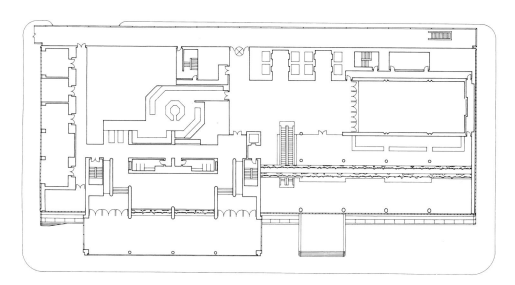

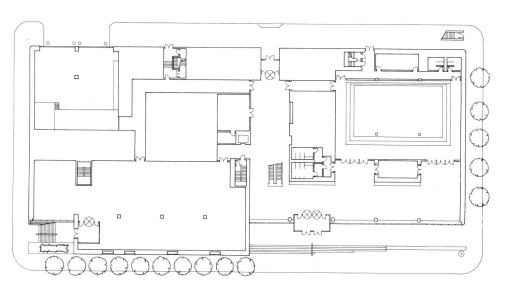

Plans (ground floor, second floor, midrise office floor).

View of the main entrance from the south- ▷ west. The glazed barrel-vaulted extension is part of the dining facility.

60'

The Menninger Foundation
Topeka, Kansas

The Menninger Foundation, a center for treatment, research and education in psychiatry, is dedicated to the treatment of the whole person in mind and body, within a caring and accepting environment. The physical facility needed to be a manifestation of that philosophy in its organization, architecture and environment. The development of a new 332-acre campus, completed in 1982, included master planning and space programming, architectural and interior design of 20 new buildings, rehabilitation of two existing facilities, and extensive landscaping.

The new complex retains the easily recognized orthogonal grid of Midwestern American towns and cities. Undulating walkways reflect the natural rise and fall of the site as they approach buildings on the diagonal, varying perspectives of form and mass. As the master plan bars automobiles from the campus, the existing tree-lined drive became a main walkway connecting patient activity centers. Covered brick walkways connect sheltered courtyards, residential quarters and related patient therapy and professional offices. Great care was taken to retain the natural beauty of the original estate. Less than five percent of the large stand of mature evergreens and shade trees were lost.

New buildings include professional offices, commons/dining, a conference center, arts and education studios, living units, and a gymnasium. The low, white-painted brick buildings incorporate a wide range of structural shapes: pitched and flat roofs, one- and two-stories, arcades, porches, atria, terraces, and garden walls. A series of courtyards binds together the new elements and redbrick older buildings. The existing tower building, a near replica of Philadelphia's Independence Hall, has become a museum and visitor center and is the focal point of the community.

The philosophy of treating patients in a community setting is reflected in the 166-bed adult psychiatric hospital spread across the brow of a hill. Early programming studies indicated the need for both integrated activities and opportunities for more private exchanges. Eight independent, one- to three-story living units grouping single and double rooms allow patients to live and interact in small groups yet be part of the larger community. Corridor window-seat alcoves offer quiet places to visit and talk. In the patient rooms, built-in furniture, natural wood ceilings and a soft-toned palette of fabrics create an inviting, comfortable atmosphere.

Site plan. ▷

120'

Partial view of the complex.

Elevation with the remodeled tower building at left.

Plan of a hospital unit. ▷

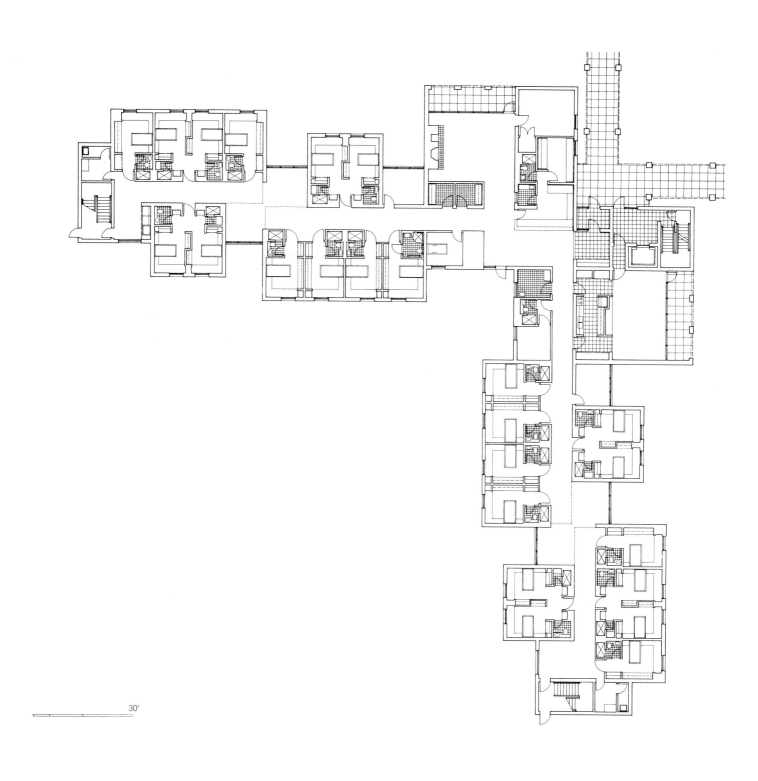

30'

A parklike setting retains the natural beauty
of the original estate.

Covered brick walkways connect courtyards,
residential quarters and the other facilities.

Fourth Financial Center
Wichita, Kansas

The nine-story headquarters building of the Fourth Financial Bank and Trust Company was completed in 1974 on the edge of a deteriorating shopping area in downtown Wichita. The client perceived this project as a catalyst to the future development of the community and wanted this first element in the planned renewal of the city's Central Business District not to be a conventional office tower but rather a unique structure generating public activity.

In addition to the bank's own facilities, the building contains rental offices on the upper floors and commercial space, a restaurant and a 200-seat meeting room on two underground levels. A glazed pedestrian bridge on the second level links the building to the downtown walkway system of the city and to a parking garage across the street. The focus of the building is a nine-story, glass-enclosed and landscaped atrium. This large atrium is oriented towards the street corner and glazed all the way up to the full building height. An Alexander Calder mobile suspended in this space underlines its vitality. The steel roof structure of the atrium is topped by a pyramidal skylight system bringing light into the center of the hall.

On the upper levels, floor areas of 33,400 square feet flank the square court in two tiers of equal length. The L-shape, with a service core at the intersection of the legs, results in excellent possibilities to subdivide the floors for use by larger or smaller tenants. Towards the south and west, offices on these floors face the atrium with window walls being at the same time protected from direct sun.

The relatively low profile of the nine-story structure is scaled to the surrounding neighborhood. As an additional advantage, the low atrium building provides smaller exterior wall surfaces, fewer elevators and a less expensive structural system than a conventional office tower. Mechanical costs and energy consumption were reduced as the interior courtyard has an insulating effect in conserving energy. While the atrium curtain wall reduces heat loss in winter, the tinted glass reduces solar heat gain in the summer, yet allows the use of natural illumination at all times during bright days.

Section.

The focus of the building is a nine-story, glass- ▷ enclosed and landscaped atrium.

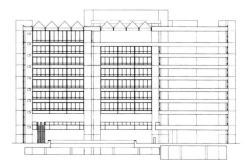

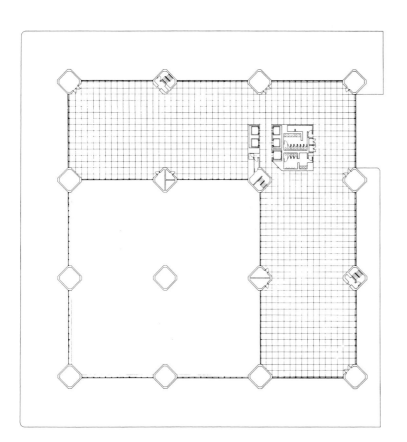

Plans (ground floor, typical floor).

View of the atrium. ▷

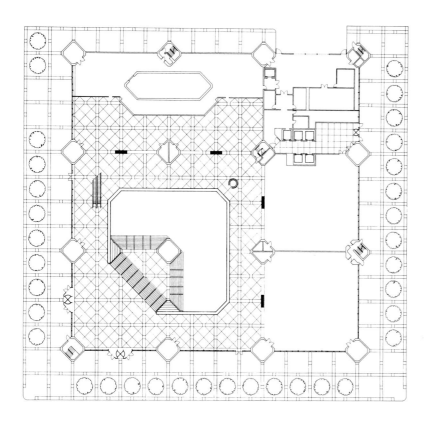

60'

Miami University Art Museum
Oxford, Ohio

The Miami University Art Museum, completed in 1979, rises from the crest of its four- to five-acre site like a sculpturesque sequence of changing architectural forms. The proportion and scale of the building elements are geometrically organized both horizontally and vertically and are highlighted by constantly changing light and shadow throughout the day.

The 24,000-square-foot museum was conceived as an active center for art and artifacts. It needed to be flexible enough to display many genres of art, and the surrounding woodlands had to be an integral part of the design. These objectives were met in a single-story barrier-free structure containing both intimate exhibit areas and large skylit spaces, as well as a 115-seat auditorium which accommodates a variety of media presentations. A reflecting pool and three exterior areas can accommodate outdoor sculpture. Through large windows and clerestories, the surroundings are visible from galleries bathed in natural light.

A small gallery, housing drawings, prints and photographs, begins a sequence of galleries adjacent to the entry lobby. Two spacious galleries reserved for larger work are followed by two intimate spaces for decorative arts and primitive works. The visitor is guided through the succession of expanding galleries by a high wall separating exhibit areas from the art storage and research areas which share natural light from the clerestories. Recesses along the wall contain media alcoves. Rear projection screens supplement exhibits and present work which cannot be installed within traditional small museums. Pocketed sliding display panels within each alcove contain additional prints and materials for study and research.

Northern clerestories in the three larger galleries rise from a flat roof, providing a wash of natural light without exposing artwork to direct sunlight. The sloped clerestory roofs are supported by exposed white-painted wooden trusses which support supplemental, moveable indoor lighting.

The entry plaza focuses on a reflecting pool and the glass-enclosed media center with moveable seats, which provide flexible space for receptions and lectures. The entry vestibule allows independent access to the media center, which is available at all times for academic and community use.

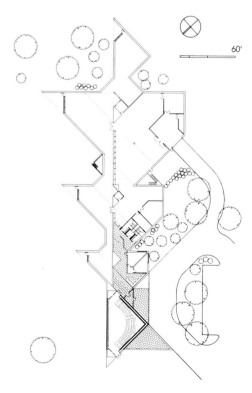

60'

◁ Plan.

In the three larger galleries northern clerestories provide a wash of natural light without exposing artwork to direct sunlight.

Pages 144–145:
The museum is situated on the crest of a gently sloping site. To the visitor the structure reveals a sequence of geometrically organized forms, highlighted by the movement of light and shadow.

Industrial Trust & Savings Bank
Muncie, Indiana

The primary consideration in designing this bank, completed in 1980, was scaling it to fit into the context of the surrounding small-scale downtown area. To respect the existing cornice heights in the area, the 52,000-square-foot building rises only three stories. The building has a dual focus. One side faces a mall with a strong pedestrian environment. The opposite orientation, from which the majority of customers arrive, is a landscaped parking area which is separated from the building by three drive-through teller stations. The geometry of the building, with its strong vertical and horizontal module, is a simple nine-part square with the center deleted to create a three-story atrium. Establishing the three floors at the same height creates the desired intimate scale at ground level. To complement both the pedestrian and parking areas, deep shadowed entries are recessed into the facade, wrapping the building in a tight glass skin.

The glass panels are interposed according to interior space uses and solar orientation. The reflective glass becomes a filter system, diminishing solar loading. The tinted glass is in the vision areas and the back-painted spandrel glass is at opaque surface areas. Each face of the building is tempered to respond to the climatic conditions of its orientation.

The massing and volume systems once defined, the interior organization was established. The original intent for the interior was to maintain the feeling of accessibility that existed in the bank's previous building. The three-story atrium space allows for this. It is open to column-free offices on three sides, with the service core on the fourth side.

In order to make the atrium a functional space and not just a lobby, the teller area was chosen to be the atrium's central focus. In contrast to the building exterior, which is subdued to integrate into the surrounding quiet community, the atrium space is defined by bands of bright colors. Orange is used in public areas along the atrium's edge, blue indicates non-public areas and red covers the walls of the core. Offices are divided by a low partition system, with glass clerestories in the upper modules. This allows for privacy yet maintains a visual awareness of the exterior surface system.

Section.

Deep shadowed entries are recessed into the ▷ facade, wrapping the building in a tight glass skin.

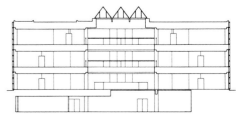

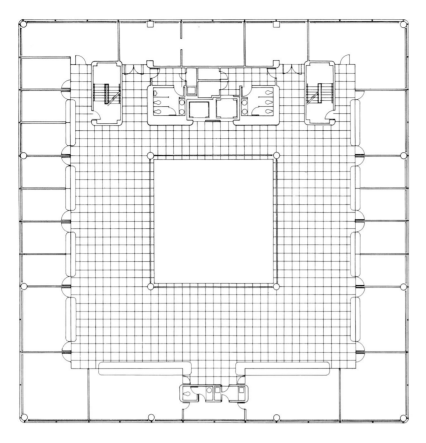

Plans (ground floor, second floor).

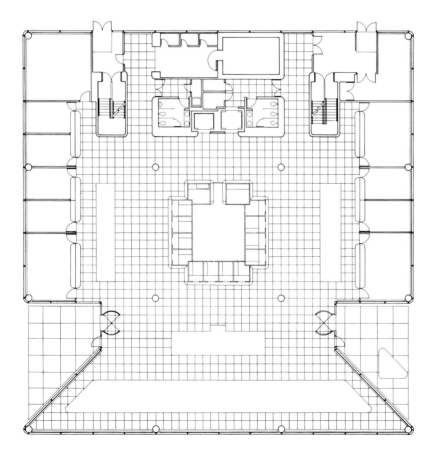

20'

Offices are divided by low partitions, with glass clerestories in the upper modules. This allows for privacy, yet a visual awareness of the exterior is maintained from all points.

Columbus City Hall
Columbus, Indiana

In 1972 SOM executed an inner-city redevelopment scheme for Columbus, a county seat south of Indianapolis, Indiana. Phased implementation of this plan has greatly enhanced the city's core area. Extending from north to south, the historic main street of this city of 38,000, Washington Street, is dominated at its southern end by the Bartholomew County Courthouse. Diagonally across from this landmark – and across from the low, glazed rectangle which SOM built for the city's daily newspaper in 1972 – is the new City Hall completed in 1981.

Columbus City Hall is a three-story building, triangular in plan with the hypotenuse forming a strong diagonal facing directly towards the Courthouse. The front presents a two-story-high, essentially opaque and monumental facade above a large lawn, which rises with a wide approach walk and steps to a glazed semi-circular entrance courtyard. Behind the glass is a circulation gallery rising full height to the second floor balcony, also a circulation gallery, and reached by stairs at each end. These two floors contain the various service departments of the city government in addition to several conference rooms, the Council Chamber on the upper floor, and an Assembly Hall at court level. The first floor is given over almost entirely to the Police Department.

It is treated as a plinth, cased in limestone and emerging out of the lawn at the front, but a full story in height on the two flanking elevations, with pierced openings onto the planted parking areas. The upper two stories, except for the entrance court, are veneered in a softly colored sand-struck brick with a tinted, wide mortar joint. The window openings are carefully proportioned with tinted glass set flush in narrow dark frames and revealed from the brick. The limestone is detailed to recall earlier attitudes towards monumental masonry. The building's structure is a composite of poured-in-place concrete (the plinth) and a light steel upper frame with steel decking and block infill behind the brick. The building is fully air-conditioned. In conclusion, the materials and most details are consistent with an adequate but austere budget. There is an ongoing civic-sponsored art program for the building.

The new City Hall in its urban context (model).

View of the main entrance. The monumental ▷ facade is approached by a wide walk with steps, which lead across a traditional "front lawn."

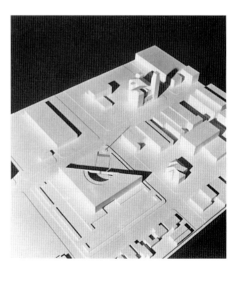

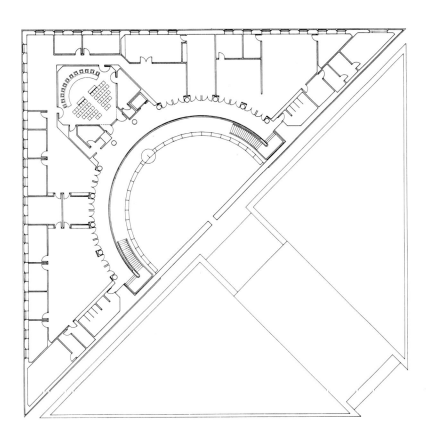

Plans (second floor, third floor).

Behind the tinted glazing of the curved court- ▷
yard wall is a large two-story gallery.

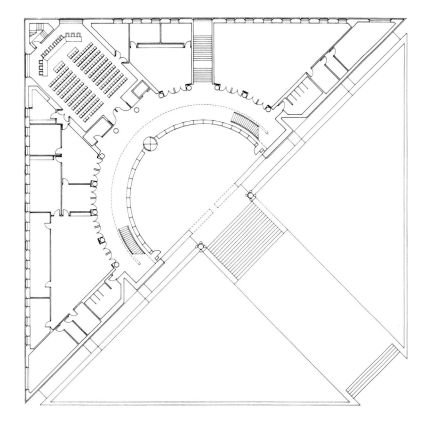

30'

2

3

4

The Southwest

During the 1970's the southwestern United States, which had long enjoyed business alliances with Chicago, New York and San Francisco, developed a north-south financial axis. Starting with Houston and New Orleans along the Gulf, the Energy Belt stretched west-northwest through Denver to Calgary in Canada. Its oil and minerals attracted American and Canadian prospectors and investors, and the Southwest saw a spectacular spurt in building. Dallas, Fort Worth, and Denver amassed dense aggregations of towers containing rentable office space. Downtown Houston leapt from SOM's 33-story Tenneco Building of the early 1960's to the 71 stories of SOM's Allied Bank Tower nearing completion in 1983.

Each of SOM's older offices has had a long and distinguished presence in the Southwest. Starting in the late 1950's, SOM/New York designed Houston's First City National Bank [2], and, in 1962, SOM/San Francisco designed the Tenneco Headquarters for the Tennessee Gas Corporation [3]. A model solar screened tower, now 20 years old, its expression of banking and office floors in articulated aluminum louvers and spandrels still commands admiration. In 1971, SOM/Chicago designed a 50-story tube-within-tube reinforced concrete structure, Houston's One Shell Plaza [4]. Led by Walter Netsch in 1955–62, SOM/Chicago addressed the awesome problems of scale, circulation and symbolism attendant upon building the U.S. Air Force Academy in the desert foothills beneath the majestic east face of the Rockies near Colorado Springs [5]. Raising its tetrahedron trusses high above the low buildings, the Chapel turns a brilliant horizontal order into a masterly expression of site. At Kitt Peak, Arizona, SOM/Chicago's Myron Goldsmith designed the National Observatory [6], and, at Austin, Texas, shortly after 1970, SOM/New York's Gordon Bunshaft designed the Lyndon Baines Johnson Library [7].

Central to those earlier SOM buildings was the intention to be monumental and emblematic. Thus SOM's Boise Cascade Headquarters in Boise, Idaho [8], is a free-standing, single mass, with a central courtyard crossed by bridges connecting peripheral offices. While wanted by the corporate client, comparable arrangements of generous but unrentable space and circulation would not be demanded by the developers who arrived in the Energy Belt in the 1970's. Rather, they sought efficient use of space and

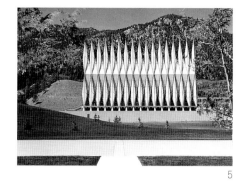

5

6

1 Skyline of Houston, Texas.
2 First City National Bank, Houston, Texas.
3 Tenneco Building, Houston, Texas.
4 One Shell Plaza, Houston, Texas.
5 U.S. Air Force Academy Chapel, Colorado, Springs, Colorado.
6 Robert R. McMath Solar Telescope, Kitt Peak National Observatory, Kitt Peak, Arizona.
7 Lyndon Baines Johnson Library, University of Texas, Austin, Texas.

7

8

9

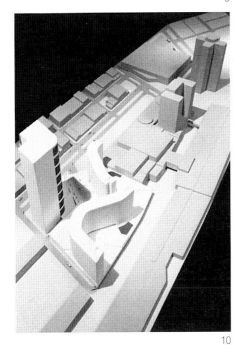

10

energy, as shown in SOM/Chicago's 28-story Pan American Life Building in New Orleans, which reduces office heights, compacts circulation, and stacks two tall atria to achieve a high ratio of floor to exterior wall. Among the remarkable designs now emanating from SOM/Denver, led by partners Kenneth Soldan and Robert Holmes, the Gulf Mineral Resources Company office buildings [9] arrange incremental units along enclosed streets, with internal skylighted atria and solar envelopes. In New Orleans, SOM/Chicago's River Center [10], 1515 Poydras [11], and One Shell Square [12] reflect their owners' concern for efficient space and economical operation. Now, instead of a corporate personality seeking an emblematic building his company would occupy, SOM was more likely to meet a team of financial managers who represented groups of investors who would occupy only a small part of a building, if any, and expected quick rentals and full return on capital. Profit lay in reducing nonrentable space, gaining additional floors, and building a marketable mixture of commercial and office space. The requirements were impersonal: the number of net rentable square feet, the dollars to be expended, and the quality of finishes and furnishings. Having begun with such requirements, as evident in Denver's Great West Plaza, SOM/Denver's designers, initially led by SOM/New York's Donald Smith, steadily won commissions for the Anaconda Building [13] and Denver National Bank [14] and by 1982 had proposed important buildings for the vital spine created by 16th and 17th Streets where Denver needs a strong architectural expression.

Measured by its individual towers, Houston is more rewarding. Seen from the west across Sam Houston Park, Houston's financial district forms a grand massif rising sheer behind open land or low public buildings. SOM's InterFirst Plaza [15], Tenneco Building, One Shell Plaza, and Allied Bank are expected to be joined by Four Houston Center [16] and Campeau Tower [17]. Nearby are towers designed by Philip Johnson and John Burgee, Ieoh Ming Pei, and Houston's CRS. Some twenty blocks of densely packed towers soar fifty and seventy stories, making one crystalline mass that is striated vertically and breaks into cubistic and faceted summits at the skyline.

In Houston, modern architects meet a city whose plan has neither a mercantile nor cultural base. Downtown Houston is built for people who drive automobiles to

11

12

13

8 Boise Cascade Home Office, Boise, Idaho.
9 Gulf Mineral Resources Headquarters, Denver, Colorado.
10 River Center, New Orleans, Louisiana.
11 1515 Poydras, New Orleans, Louisiana.
12 One Shell Square, New Orleans, Louisiana.
13 Anaconda Building, Denver, Colorado.

14

15

offices where they work with messages. Their world has manifest dependencies on oil and electricity for its physical energy and on money and risk for its psychic energy. Companies have made extraordinary provisions for their employees, not only in work space, but in recreational space, notably Tenneco's new Employee Benefits Center [18], designed by SOM/Houston's Richard Keating in 1982. The office towers speak of the need to manage time efficiently, expressed in garages, fast elevators, computers, and push-button access, and the need to display competence and success, expressed in prestigious addresses, club memberships, art-filled conference rooms and generous lobbies. The tower then is given a distinctive summit, and the summits are emblems of identity and prestige.

That the architectural result can be elegant has been demonstrated repeatedly in towers sponsored by the forceful, enlightened developer, Houston's Gerald Hines, who built Houston's One Shell Plaza and thereafter a succession of buildings that meet both financial and aesthetic measures. Among the five towers in Houston designed by SOM, Hines' InterFirst Plaza is clearly a masterpiece. Buoyant, generous and cheerful, its generosity starts with a large plaza, cascades interior offices in the airy banking lobby, and ends in an exuberant almost incandescent summit, the whole being the brilliant concept of San Francisco's Lawrence Doane and Edward C. Bassett. Hines' leadership and InterFirst Plaza's success encouraged other developers. Now, with Tenneco, InterFirst and One Shell Plaza in place, developer Kenneth Schnitzer asked SOM to propose a tower for Allied Bank [19]. Designed by Houston partner Keating in collaboration with San Francisco partner Bassett, the tower is as unexpected as it is successful: a 71-story turning point in Houston's western skyline. Formed by two quarter cylinders, the slender glazed shaft juxtaposes curves and straight planes that play with light and reflections even at street level, where, seen against the background of InterFirst or One Shell, the dark green shaft marks a sharp apostrophe to their complex forms.

Still, however fine each tower may be, the Energy Belt cities lack downtown urban districts that support residents' needs for more than office space. New Orleans often succeeds in mixing markets, residence, work, recreation, and education. By 1980, Denver seemed to be awakening, but there was less assurance that Houston had. SOM's Houston and Denver offices were

16

17

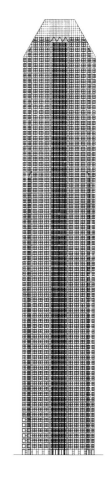

14 Denver National Bank, Denver, Colorado.
15 InterFirst Plaza, Houston, Texas.
16 Four Houston Center, Houston, Texas.
17 Campeau Tower, Houston, Texas.

18

only beginning to be asked to address some of those cities' urban problems. Both cities might well refer to the San Antonio River Corridor Study [20] SOM/San Francisco completed in 1973. Impelled by the need for flood control, that Study proposed a six-mile stretch of new residential and commercial districts in recreational parks, an urban ideal that Energy Belt cities should be encouraged to emulate.

19

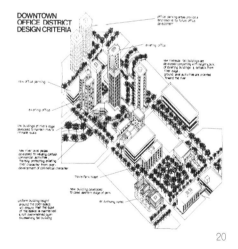

20

18 Tenneco Employee Center, Houston, Texas.
19 Allied Bank Plaza, Houston, Texas.
20 Study on the San Antonio River Corridor,
   San Antonio, Texas.

InterFirst Plaza
Houston, Texas

The 55-story office tower of the First International Corporation in Houston is clad in polished rose-colored granite combined with matching reflective glass. The building is 748 feet tall and contains a total gross area of 1.9 million square feet, of which 1.2 million is rentable office and commercial space. Each typical floor of the steel and concrete composite framed tube has a net usable area of approximately 22,000 square feet.

The building is adjacent to Tenneco, designed by SOM in 1963, Shell by SOM in 1971, and just several streets from the First National Bank of Houston by SOM in 1961.

Approach to the building entrance is on the northeast side by way of a plaza with a large Dubuffet polychromed sculpture.

The tower has climate-controlled underground access across the street to the adjacent hotel with its restaurants and convention facilities as well as to a 1,500-car parking garage just to the west. These pedestrian walkways are part of an extensive tunnel system between almost every major building in downtown Houston, required by the adverse climatic conditions of the Southwest.

To the southeast, the banking hall is placed at an angle to the tower, which is bevelled in various ways as it rises. On this side a sawtooth pattern is carried up the entire height, resulting in a multitude of desirable corner offices. The tower wall configuration is repeated in the treatment of the hall's roof. The bevelled exterior wall which forms the envelope on this side of the tower extends down unchanged to flank the bank lobby. Supported by girders 15 feet in height, the roof of the hall steps down in a pyramid of levels from north to south, where a maximum span of about 162 feet is reached. Linear skylights fill the horizontal intervals between the Z-shaped girders, and a large northern window wall faces the plaza.

The building is air-conditioned with the most advanced systems of controls and security, including the electronic dispatching for the tower's 27 passenger elevators.

Section through the banking hall and tower elevation.

In spite of its location in the heart of down- ▷
town Houston, the tower enjoys unobstructed views.

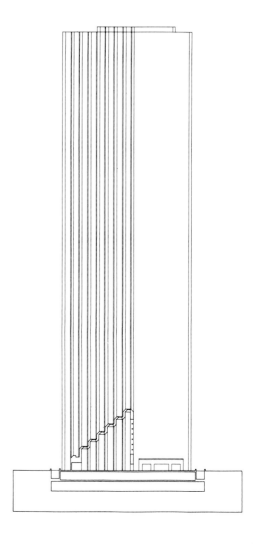

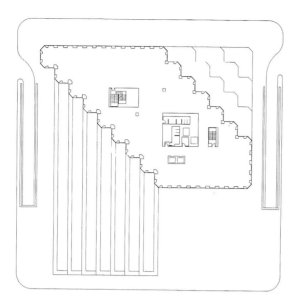

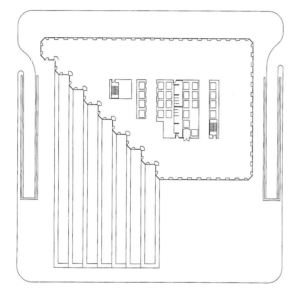

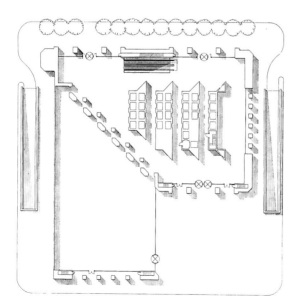

Plans (ground floor, typical floor, top floor).

The faceted angles of the tower's southeast ▷ wall reflect the intense southern sunlight in a very lively way.

60'

Allied Bank Plaza
Houston, Texas

The 71-story Allied Bank Plaza in downtown Houston, under construction since 1980, is directly adjacent to three other SOM buildings: the Tenneco Building to the east, One Shell Plaza to the north and First International Plaza to the south.

Allied Bank commands its own identity through its distinctive design, yet also complements and ties together its surroundings. By forcing the site west, SOM created a linear open space along Louisiana Street. East, across Smith Street, the scale of the downtown business district gives rise to Allied Bank – dramatizing its prominence.

The tower was conceived as a bundled tube, rising without setbacks, over a plan formed by two quarter-circles. A sequence of steel columns, set at 15-foot on center, follows the round and rectangular plan and is so effective structurally that no additional interior columns or bracing walls in the core section are required. The typical floor areas of 25,000 gross square feet allow flexible space planning.

Allied Bank is sheathed in a curtain wall of energy efficient, high insulating blue-green reflective glass. An overall grid of dark green vertical and horizontal mullions and vertical stainless steel window-washing tracks at the column lines subtly express the structural system and give scale to the huge expanses of glass.

The main entrance to Allied Bank, on Louisiana Street, is connected to Houston's climate-controlled underground tunnel system at a large landscaped plaza area which features a fountain.

View of the 71-story tower (model).

Plans (ground level, typical floor). ▷

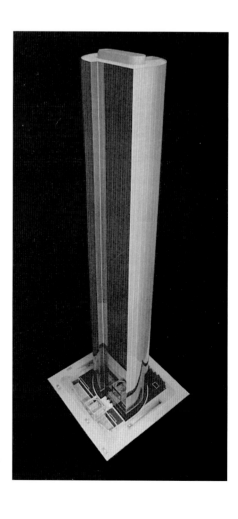

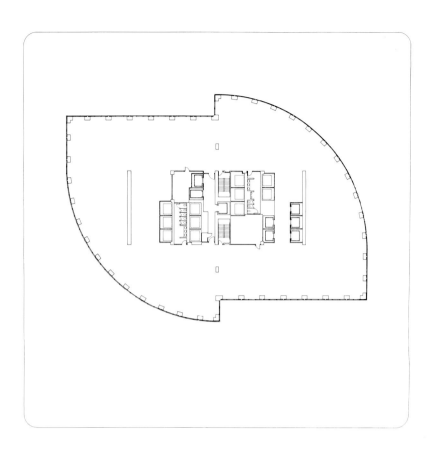

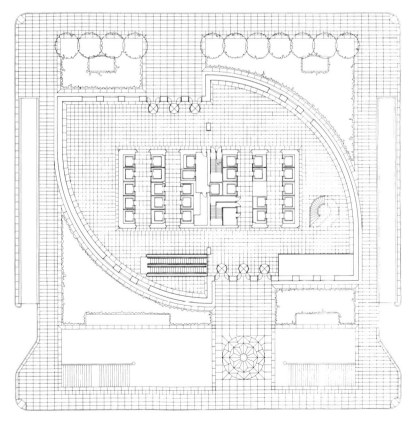

30'

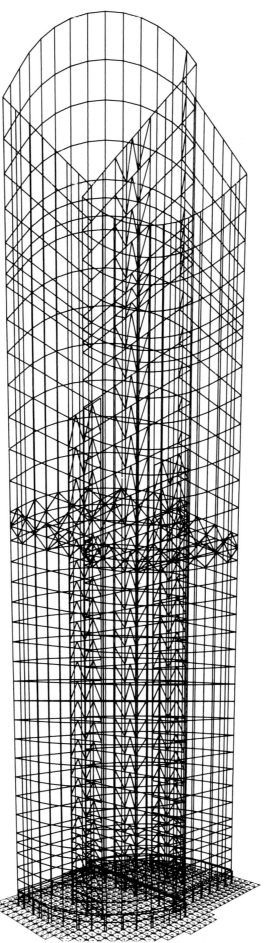

Three SOM-designed towers on Houston's
skyline: One Shell Plaza, Allied Bank Plaza
and InterFirst Plaza (photomontage).

Study on the San Antonio River Corridor
San Antonio, Texas

The San Antonio River is both the geographic and the spiritual heart of the 250-year-old city of San Antonio, Texas. It flows through established residential neighborhoods as well as by historic buildings, including fragments of original Spanish settlements. 20 feet below street level, the river winds through a downtown which is the regional center for more than a million persons.

In 1972 and 1973 SOM, in joint venture with Marshall Kaplan Gans and Kahn, established a development program that used flood control improvements together with a variety of related public and private investments to make the river a catalyst for downtown revitalization. The total study area encompasses more than 3,000 acres surrounding a six-mile segment of the river. The plan develops specific policies and programs which treat the river as a unique and historic asset for residents and tourists, the downtown as a regional center with inner-city neighborhoods, and an administrative body as a framework for both decision making and managing corridor revitalization.

At the regional scale, modifications to freeways and streets and other public transit recommendations make the central area more accessible. Because economic growth in the downtown is not unlimited, a principal recommendation at the project scale is to carefully locate new development so that it can maximize beneficial land uses and take advantage of the new river amenity and pedestrian environment.

Neighborhood revitalization is based on the introduction of new and rehabilitated housing in parallel with improvements in education and other inner-city community facilities. New high-density sites and neighborhood centers are located in relation to inner landscape improvements. The newly landscaped river becomes an attraction for new residents and a gathering place for neighborhood services.

In order to insure that plan goals are implemented, a decision framework is developed which provides a recommended new agency, the Office of River Corridor Development, with a methodology for evaluating project proposals and accommodating citizen input. The greatest virtue of the plan is its ability to combine existing activities, historical assets and newly proposed open space and recreation areas.

Regional plan.
1 San Antonio River Corridor study area

The "dream" plan which summarizes the ▷ study's goals for rehabilitation of the river and 3,000 acres of land that surround it.
1 Flood control
2 Open space/recreation
3 Access
4 CBD retail
5 CBD office
6 Visitor services
7 Internal circulation
8 Housing

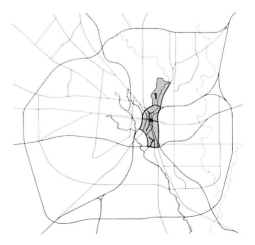

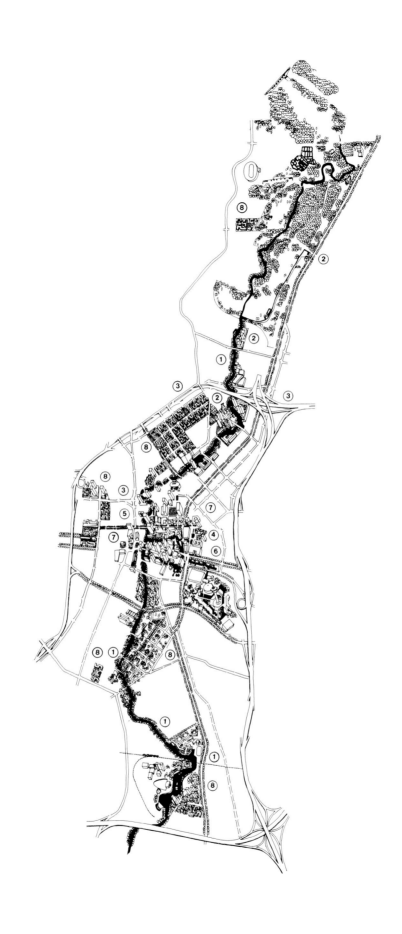

Lone Star Gardens

Roosevelt Park

bike path

promenade

ROOSEVELT LANDING

section 1

River sections. The natural potential and resources provided by the existing river will be put to use to transform the environment as a place of recreation and a site for attractive urban housing.

The plan of the environmental form which shows the impact of existing features on the plan.

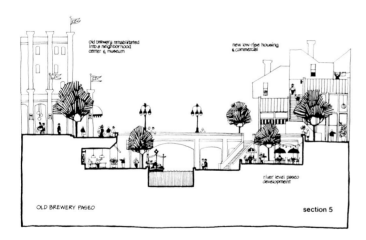

neighborhood park

bike path

riverside linear park

RIVERSIDE PARK NEAR FIFTH STREET

section 4

Old brewery rehabilitated into a neighborhood center & museum

new low-rise housing & commercial

river level paseo development

OLD BREWERY PASEO

section 5

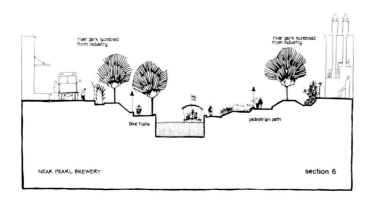

river park screened from industry

river park screened from industry

bike trails

pedestrian path

NEAR PEARL BREWERY

section 6

Aerial view of the San Antonio River looking toward the Central Business District.

Amenities including commercial and recreational areas line the river.

The East Coast

2

3

In early Spring 1982, the intersection of Park Avenue with 52nd and 53rd Streets gained new expanse and light. The midblock Park Avenue Plaza [2] set 45-degree angles to Manhattan's orthogonal grid and gave Park Avenue a different scale. A speculative investment by Fisher Brothers, the 44-story tower gained a few extra stories by providing a block-wide enclosed plaza and was quickly leased in a strong market for midtown office space close to Grand Central Station and corporate headquarters. Remarkably, the Plaza is also a successful aesthetic form. Its base strikes the Racquet Club's cornice; its eastern chamfer squares with the Seagram Tower; notches in its four-bay half chamfers resolve dualities; and its reflectivities receive Lever House. Beyond those acknowledgments to important neighbors, the Plaza's designer, SOM/New York's Raul de Armas, created a new lateral focus, broadening Park Avenue's corridor. Handsomely faceted, the Plaza's deformations denote a perimetal tubular frame and central columnar core. Neither structural nor mechanical expression mars its glistening, bevelled surfaces which end at the skyline without cornice or transition save the jagged silhouette of the crystal itself.

The happy congruence of Park Avenue Plaza and the New York Racquet and Tennis Club dramatizes nearly a century of Manhattan's architectural history, which turned from McKim, Mead & White's Renaissance imagery to the modern forms of SOM's Lever House [3]. The transformation was owed to many architects, but the seminal and purest advocate of modern urban corporate architecture was SOM/ New York's Gordon Bunshaft, designer of Lever House. His 1954 Manufacturers Hanover Trust Building on Fifth Avenue at 43rd Street and his 1960 Pepsi Cola Building at 500 Park Avenue, corner of 59th Street, are glazed pavilions notable for fine proportions and refined detail. His Beinecke Library at Yale University is much more than an exhibition of translucent marble held in a precast concrete frame: its siting and cubic, angular silhouette wed it to the Gothic Revival and Beaux Arts buildings bordering its plaza. Retired in 1979, Bunshaft instilled his sense of dramatic scale and refined detail on younger partners Gordon Wildermuth, Donald Smith, Raul de Armas and Michael McCarthy. For the government of Kuwait,

4

1 Skyline of New York, New York.
2 Park Avenue Plaza, New York, New York.
3 Lever House, New York, New York.
4 Chase Manhattan Bank, New York, New York.
5 Union Carbide Building, New York, New York.

5

6 Emhart Corporation Headquarters, Bloomfield, Connecticut.
7 American Can Headquarters, Greenwich, Connecticut.
8 General Electric Headquarters, Fairfield, Connecticut.
9 Texaco Headquarters, Harrison, New York.
10 Trailways Bus Terminal, Boston, Massachusetts.

8

McCarthy drew the exquisite Kuwait Chancery in Washington, D.C., where precision, formality and elegance stand in SOM's best tradition.

During the three decades between Lever House and Park Avenue Plaza, it was not certain that America's northeastern cities would regain vitality. SOM's One Liberty Plaza for U.S. Steel was built near Wall Street, but many national manufacturing companies fled New York City. The Chase Manhattan Bank's decision to build SOM's building [4] downtown was exceptional at a time when major banks were moving midtown. In 1982, Manufacturers Hanover Trust bought the Park Avenue headquarters Union Carbide [5] vacated, and SOM was recalled to remodel the building it had designed in the late 1950's.

Accelerating throughout the 1970's, the drive to suburban and rural locations was led by senior officers' preference for having their headquarters on meadow and forested land near highways and small airports. In the 1960's, SOM had designed rural headquarters for Emhart Manufacturing [6], Armstrong Cork, Reynolds Metal, and American Can [7]. Now, in the 1970's, SOM gave General Electric a pair of buildings on a steep site bordering the Merritt Parkway in Fairfield, Connecticut [8]. Westinghouse received a frontispiece for its existing factories, and Texaco gained a headquarters [9] that is exemplary for its insolation and arboreal gardens.

Before eastern cities could reverse the exodus, several urban problems had to be overcome, beginning with transportation. Guided by SOM/Boston, Massachusetts' Governor was advised to abandon plans for an eight-lane road beneath Boston's Harbor and, instead, to tunnel only a two-lane road to connect buses and limousines from Boston to Logan Airport and the growing northern communities. The study also urged that money intended for an eight-mile road completing circumferential 495 should be diverted to Boston's subway and surface transit. Led by Boston partner Peter Hopkinson, SOM/Boston designed Boston's Trailways Bus Terminal [10] and redesigned the congested BMTA station at Cambridge's Harvard Square [11]. Meanwhile SOM/Washington studied the rail lines in the Northeast Corridor [12]. Still wary of waterways, Americans kept an unrequited faith in railroads, and the Federal Government now sponsored an extensive study led by SOM/Washington partner David Childs. Boston's South Station

6

7

9

10

11

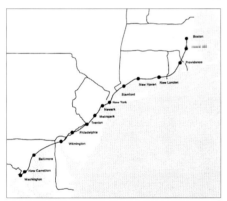

12

13

14

[13] would see its tracks redirected to arrive at a new concourse embraced by the restored and reconstructed old head-house. Providence, with its delaying curve straightened, would gain a new station [14] with a low dome echoing Charles F. McKim's nearby State Capitol. The stations at New London, New Haven and Newark were to be remodelled, and Wilmington's old station [15], which the fanciful Frank Furness had designed, would be given a new interior and plaza. Each step was encumbered, but the improvements encouraged hope for greater rail use.

While American downtown railroad stations did not yet confirm Canadian cities' success in generating commercial investment, American cities' major subway interchanges did attract such development. Near New York's World Trade Center, the first modern hotel in New York's financial district, the Vista Hotel [16] by SOM/New York partners Donald Smith and Leon Moed, opened in 1982 at the Center's southwest corner. At the juncture of G Street with 12th and 13th Streets in Washington's retail district, Metro Center [17] started an immediate and predicted demand for rental space. Seeing that opportunity, developer Oliver T. Carr, Jr. retained SOM/Washington to plan three blocks along G Street. Reminiscent of Washington's classical buildings, Childs' proposal envisages sympathetic bays and inflections and achieves remarkable urban open space.

One of several exceptional features in Metro Center is its skillful juxtaposition of the new with the old and preserved. Similarly, SOM/Washington terraced an office building over the one-bay deep facades of houses at 1777 F Street [18]. In Metropolitan Square [19], two Beaux Arts buildings, the Keith Albee Theater and the National Metropolitan Bank, were engaged into a new building and joined with the existing Garfinkle's Department Store, the resulting complex filling a city block punctuated by SOM's central glass-covered atrium. In Boston, SOM/Boston's plan for Commonwealth Pier V [20] restores buildings on half the pier, while the other half is to be cleared for an office building and hotel. Again in Boston, SOM/Chicago's tall Sixty State Street [21] on the irregular site near Faneuil Hall and the Old State House reserves sixty percent of its site for a plaza and restores the previously closed vistas to Faneuil Hall and the Old State House. Such historic and spatial references were seldom absent. Miami was exceptional.

15

16

17

18

11 Harvard Square Station, Cambridge, Massachusetts.
12 Northeast Corridor with Boston – Washington railway line.
13 Boston South Station, Boston, Massachusetts.
14 Providence Station, Providence, Rhode Island.
15 Wilmington Station, Wilmington, Delaware.
16 Vista International Hotel, New York, New York.
17 Metro Center, Washington, D.C.
18 1777 F Street, Washington, D.C.

17

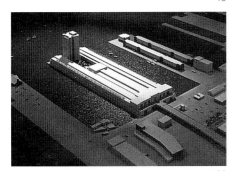

19

20

21

22

On Brickell Avenue, SOM/New York's Interterra Building [22], like SOM/San Francisco's Southeast Financial Center [23], attempts to establish a new form. Designed by New York partner Donald Smith, the Interterra Building introduces landscape, shops and apartments in an office building on a tree-lined boulevard that has been rapidly disfigured by disparate buildings and empty plazas. Southeast Financial Center, designed by SOM/San Francisco partner Bassett, is meant to be seen in the round, two buildings connected by a glazed canopy; the tower's cascade of bays creates southeastern corner offices facing Bay Front Park and Key Biscayne.

More often, a medley of influences affected buildings' form. In Manhattan, limitations on land coverage and floor area ratios suggested that 9 West 57th Street [24], completed in 1973, take shape as a swoop-curved slab, devote 30 percent of its midblock site to a plaza, and cover only 40 percent of its site from its nineteenth floor upwards, expressed in a thin slab with exposed steel windbracing. A variant is the 50-story 780 Third Avenue [25], between 48th and 49th Streets, expected to be completed in 1983. Its concrete tube rises from only 40 percent of its site, resulting in a tall slender tower whose diagonal windbracing is expressed in granite wall patterns. In Atlanta, the Georgia-Pacific Center [26], completed in 1982, acknowledges Margaret Mitchell Square and accents the intersection of Peachtree and Houston Streets. When such formal determinants converge in a design that seems inevitable, architects exult in their confluence. Such is the happy air surrounding SOM/New York's Irving Trust Operations Center [27], located in lower Manhattan north of the World Trade Center. The trapezoidal site, combining of two city blocks, conversion of the intervening street into an atrium, and joining of two separate buildings, one for Irving Trust's operations, the other for rental offices, were resolved by SOM/New York partner Raul de Armas within a low cube that boasts compactness, energy efficiency, natural light, and a dramatic conclusion to urban vistas.

SOM's work in the eastern United States displays exceptional talent in strengthening the character and performance of worn urban areas. Two special examples in Washington reveal the skill, simplicity and restraint exercised by SOM/Washington partners David Childs and Walter Arensberg. For the Bicentennial, SOM/Washington restored

23

19 Metropolitan Square, Washington, D.C.
20 Plan for Commonwealth Pier V, Boston, Massachusetts.
21 Sixty State Street, Boston, Massachusetts.
22 Interterra Building, Miami, Florida.
23 Southeast Financial Center, Miami, Florida.
24 9 West 57th Street, New York, New York.

24

25

the Mall's central axis [28], removed automobiles from Washington and Adams Drives, planted elm canopies, made pedestrian paths, and bordered them with appropriate furnishings. Thereafter, SOM/Washington created Constitution Gardens [29] on the 52 acres between the Reflecting Pool and Constitution Avenue. Gently sloped meadows, shade trees, and a six-acre lake, all connected by meandering paths, are arranged to accent views towards the Lincoln Memorial and Washington Monument. Those great monuments of American history are dignified and dramatized by the Gardens, which were modestly and surely developed in the classical tradition of natural landscape.

28

29

26

25 780 Third Avenue, New York, New York.
26 Georgia-Pacific Center, Atlanta, Georgia.
27 Irving Trust Operations Center, New York, New York.
28 The Mall, Washington, D.C.
29 Constitution Gardens, Washington, D.C.

27

Park Avenue Plaza
New York, New York

Park Avenue Plaza, situated behind the New York Racquet and Tennis Club in the heart of the city, was completed in 1981. Forty-one office floors totaling approximately 25,000 square feet each surmount a 30-foot-high interior plaza with a retail area and mezzanine lobby.

Because of the building's 1,000,000-square-foot volume, it was designed to respond sensitively to its urban setting, specifically the adjacent McKim, Mead & White Racquet Club and the nearby Lever House and Mies van der Rohe's Seagram Building. This was accomplished in a number of ways: an angled geometric shape with chamfered corners and notched sides minimizes the building's bulk and recedes from the Racquet Club; tinted green glass sheathing with silvery mullions reflects the sky, relates to neighboring Park Avenue facades, and relieves the weight of the tower; the traditional street wall is maintained in a base which is flush with adjacent buildings; and the base of the tower continues the cornice line of the Racquet Club. An initial scheme distributed the volume at three levels to correspond with the heights of surrounding buildings. However, modifications in the client's program called for maximum floor area to be built for each story.

Soaring glass walls frame the indoor plaza, creating a feeling of light, air and spaciousness. Beyond the revolving glass doors, three-story-high columns clad in stainless steel and green polished marble walls define an enormous skylighted through-block public space enhanced by a 50-foot-wide waterfall, greenery, tables and chairs, and a pair of green painted glass kitchen kiosks serving restaurant patrons. This through-block arcade provides more amenities than the zoning resolution requires. The smaller shopping arcade recalls the intimacy of a variety of shops along narrow European streets. A sense of natural light is created overhead, while the merchandise is spotlighted at eye level in the rounded bay windows. The shops relate to the public space through the continuous use of similar materials and details, such as clear and very dark tinted green glass, stainless steel and polished bronze. Escalators transport tenants and visitors from the street level to the lobby mezzanine where they board tower elevators. This area has been carefully planned to assure both unity of design and maximum security.

Elevation.

View of the office tower across Park Avenue. ▷ The new building sensitively respects its urban context with an angled geometry and a reflecting curtain wall minimizing the building's bulk.

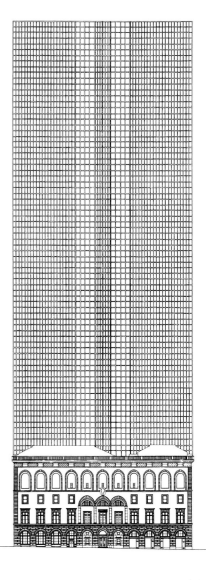

Plans (ground floor, typical floor).

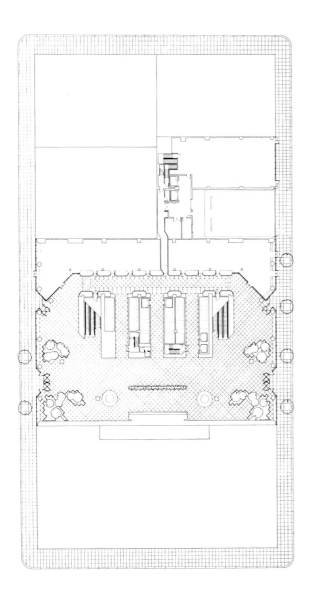
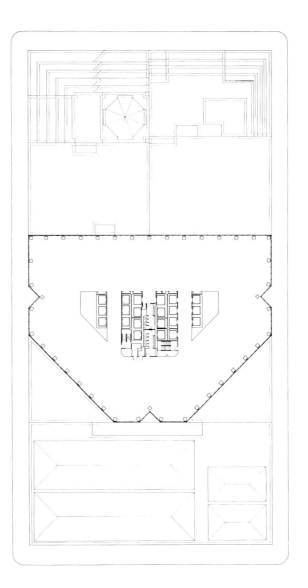

30'

18

Irving Trust Operations Center
New York, New York

The design of the Irving Trust Company's operations center in New York City evolved from a response to the site, special Washington Street Urban Renewal District requirements, and programmatic needs of the bank. The two-acre site is located two blocks from the World Trade Center in lower Manhattan's densely built and populated financial district. A portion of Washington Street was closed, combining two city blocks into a trapezoidal plot.

The closed street became the footprint for a 60-foot-wide atrium which divides the structure into 23- and 16-story sections. Floors 17 through 23 in the 1,156,000-square-foot building will be leased until Irving Trust requires the additional floors for expansion. The steel frame structure, to be completed in 1983, is enclosed entirely with 6-foot-by-4-foot glass panels. A polychromatic, ribboned effect is created by the use of three different types of glass. Partially reflective and clear vision glass bands wrap the building between white opaque glass spandrel panels. The partially reflective glass permits light to enter without glare, and therefore is positioned above the transparent, or vision, glass, set at eye level. Secondary light enters the atrium and penetrates interior glazed walls, so that an employee is never more than 45 feet from natural light and a view. The atrium also conserves energy, as one-third of the perimeter of the floor space is not subjected to the sun's direct heat, thereby reducing the air-conditioning load on adjacent office space.

Due to the technical nature of an operations center, virtually every desk can be equipped with a cathode-ray terminal. Because employees will spend a large portion of their day working on machines, the management felt it was necessary to provide space for employee interaction and relaxation. A landscaped cafeteria and lounge area will overlook the atrium from the top floor of the 16-story section beneath long span sloping steel trusses with clerestory windows.

General view from the southeast. ▷

Section.

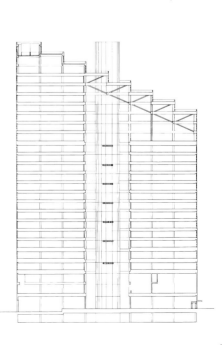

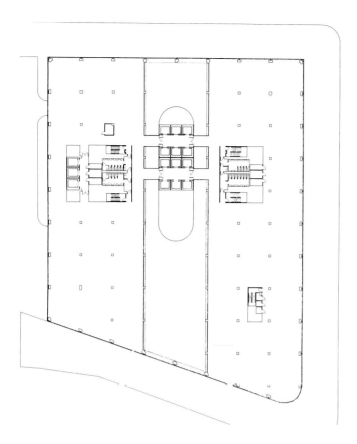

Plans (ground floor, typical floor).

View of the cafeteria and lounge area. ▷

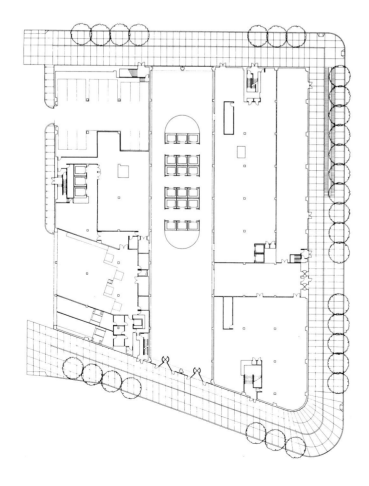

30′

780 Third Avenue
New York, New York

A 50-story commercial office tower, 780 Third Avenue is currently under construction between 48th and 49th Streets in Manhattan. The 470,000-square-foot tower, occupying a 22,092-square-foot site, is scheduled for completion in 1983.

Due to the building's unusual height-to-slenderness ratio, a concrete tube system was selected. The structure is braced diagonally and distributes the wind load equally among perimeter columns. The pattern of alternating red polished granite panels and gray-tinted insulating glass windows reveals the structural system. The interiors, as a result, are column-free and will provide flexible tenant space.

The design of the rectangular tower is in part a response to the New York City zoning resolution, which, prior to its amendment in 1982, allowed a building occupying 40 percent of its site to maximize the allowable floor area ratio. This stipulation permitted the design of a tall, slender tower – the floor plate is only 8,836 square feet, while the tower is over 550 feet tall.

At ground level, the plaza will be landscaped with trees, fountains, lights, and benches.

Aerial view of 780 Third Avenue.

Elevations (east, north, west, south). ▷

Plan (typical floor).

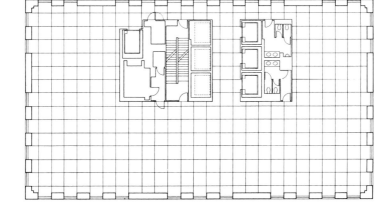

15'

Headquarters of Alexander & Alexander
New York, New York

The headquarters of this major insurance company occupies one floor in the Celanese Building on the Avenue of the Americas in midtown Manhattan. This interior design project, totalling 35,000 square feet, was completed in 1978. When Alexander & Alexander considered the decor of its corporate offices, the desire was to create a warm, personal environment for employees, clients and visitors. Art was considered crucial in achieving this, thus leading to the selection of nearly 100 separate pieces of art from around the world. On display in hallways, galleries, offices and rooms are works from America, Africa, India, China and other countries. The common idea in the selection of pieces was that most were created by people for actual use in their daily lives.

The Chairman of the Board's executive office is finished with teak floors and floor-to-ceiling lacquered screens at the windows. The interior walls are covered with handwoven linen framed in bronze. A mid-nineteenth-century Kashmir shawl is the focal work of art. A contemporary desk with marble top and bronze base is positioned near an antique Oriental rug.

The bog oak conference table in the room adjacent to the president's office is trimmed with bronze blades and surrounded by eight chairs upholstered in suede. The floor is teak and the walls are of teak veneer and bronze-trimmed, handwoven linen. The artwork is highlighted by a lone star Mennonite quilt and a Chinese junk circa 1825–50.

The executive dining room is a mixture of old and new. The glass and polished bronze dining table is flanked by twelve Queen Anne chairs. An unusual collection of artwork includes a red lacquer Thai teak bull and Yoruba twin figures. On one wall, again covered with handwoven linen, hang fifteen ceremonial weapons from the South Seas.

Plan.

Reception area. ▷

President's office.

Executive dining room.

30'

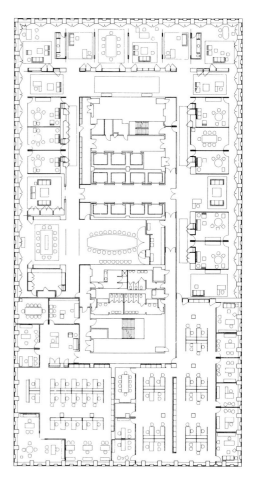

Headquarters of the Continental Grain Company
New York, New York

Since their move to midtown Manhattan in 1975, the Continental Grain Company headquarters has occupied 117,039 square feet on the 8th, 35th, and 48th through 50th floors of 277 Park Avenue. Perimeter offices on the typical floors vary from 10 feet by 15 feet, to 15 feet by 15 feet, to 15 feet by 20 feet. Each office affords a wide view of the city as well as a view of the interior reception gallery through floor-to-ceiling glass partitions. The executive 50th floor has nine offices, three conference rooms, a boardroom and an executive dining room.

Careful attention was given to the selection of materials, textures and colors. The floors are travertine, the core wall is covered in sisal trimmed in polished bronze, and the boardroom and dining room are enclosed in bronze tinted glass. Lacquered wood sun screens were chosen rather than conventional drapery. The elevator and office doors and structural columns are polished bronze and a polished bronze spiral staircase leads from the main reception area to the floor below.

Works of art have been generously used to complement an atmosphere of subtle luxury. Modern etchings, aquatints, lithographs, and serigraphs, as well as paintings in oil and acrylic, tapestries and both primitive and modern sculptures are on view.

Plan (50th floor).

View of the reception area with spiral stair- ▷ case leading to the floor below.

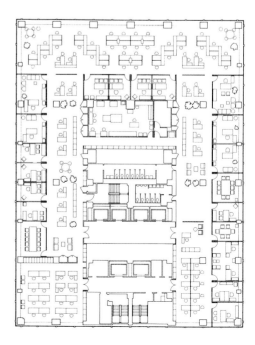

194

Vista International Hotel
New York, New York

The Vista International Hotel at the World Trade Center in New York City was originally designed with 450 rooms in the late 1960's. A foundation and three levels were built before the owner's program was substantially increased due to the dynamic growth of the lower Manhattan market. When SOM became involved in 1978, their commission was to build an 825-room hotel on the preexisting base. The 24-story steel frame building was completed in 1981.

The service level includes administrative offices, training facilities, and parking. Directly above, the lobby level, which is accessible from the street and the trade center concourse, includes check-in facilities, shops, and the ballroom. Off the trade center plaza, the plaza level contains the balance of the hotel's important public spaces: the business center with secretarial and communication services; two restaurants; and an expansive lounge. Because the hotel is located in a major financial district, a need for special facilities to serve an international investment community existed. While floors 4–19 contain guestrooms, the third floor is reserved for conference facilities with 12 conference rooms and a lounge, and floors 20–21 are used for the VIP Club. The Executive Fitness Center with a pool and racquetball courts, occupies the top two levels.

In order to minimize the weight of the new structure, a steel frame rather than the originally planned concrete was selected. This enabled the engineers to increase the height of the hotel to 22 stories above the Trade Center plaza. Wind loading was also a problem as the hotel was constructed in one of the windiest places in the nation, and the solution required much heavier wind bracing than normally found in a 22-story building.

The first architect envisioned a dark anodized aluminum skin to match the other low-rise buildings in the complex. Given the increased bulk of the hotel, a light anodized skin, in the same design vocabulary as the two towers, was selected as more appropriate. Horizontal strips of glass and aluminum panels were used to contrast with the tower's vertically expressed skin, and to maintain the hotel's own architectural identity.

Site plan with typical hotel floor.

View of the Vista International Hotel with the ▷ World Trade Center across the Hudson River.

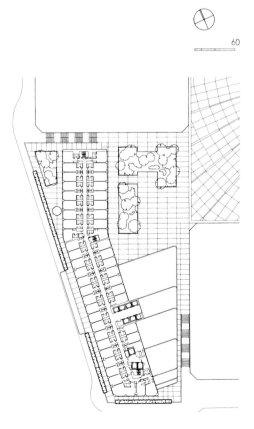

60

Restaurants and lounges are located at the plaza level adjacent to the Trade Center Plaza. The Greenhouse restaurant, enclosed in a two-story glass structure, provides an outstanding dining environment.

The building is clad with a light anodized aluminum skin.

Headquarters of Texaco
Harrison, New York

The Texaco corporate headquarters, completed in 1978, was built at a secluded location in a low-density residential neighborhood on the suburban fringe of New York City. The triangular 107-acre site is bordered by two expressways and a major street. The travertine clad, concrete building totals 1,156,000 square feet and can accommodate 2,100 employees. A terrace level houses mechanical equipment and personnel services, including a cafeteria, above which three office floors are stepped back around interior courtyards. A two-floor underground parking garage holds 1,500 cars.

The most important considerations in determining the conceptual design were the zoning restrictions, scale of the neighboring residential area, vehicular access and parking, and efforts to conserve both energy and the natural landscape. The solution was a single building centrally located on the site. The single building concept reduced the disturbance to the landscape, and the central location shielded the building from the neighboring community. Parking was located beneath and in front of the building; the roof deck was landscaped as a grassy forecourt containing a circular entrance drive.

The long axis was positioned east-west in order to reduce the sun load on the tinted thermal glazing, which is also shielded by a 9-foot overhang. Floor-to-ceiling glazing is thus possible within the constraints of energy conservation, enabling the occupants to enjoy an unobstructed view of the natural landscape.

The interior terraced courtyards were planned for the enjoyment of the employees. Provision has also been made for the creation of a pond, a system of nature trails, and a dining area on the lawn outside the cafeteria.

Space planning was a major concern for the development of a program of 750,000 square feet of interior office space. A workstation concept evolved with four enclosed office types and five open area workstations. The workstations were developed into a flexible system for planning, the goal being to provide the client with a single open planning system that could be implemented without professional assistance in the future.

Plan (typical floor).

Site plan. ▷

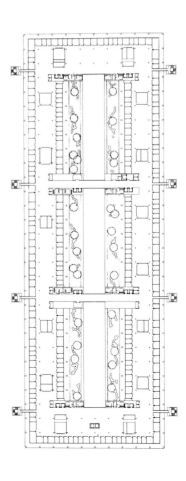

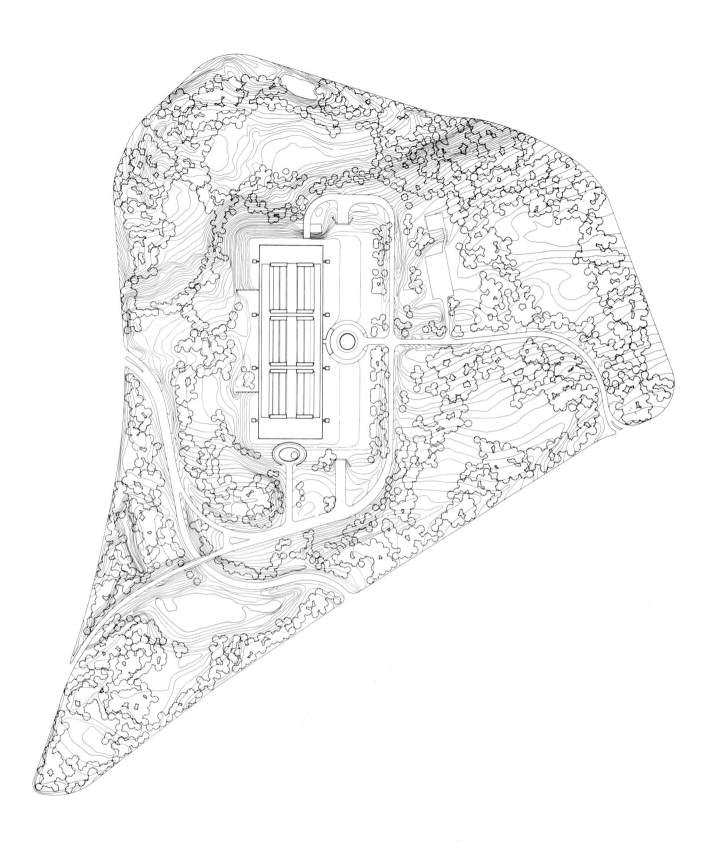

300'

Aerial view. The 107-acre site is bordered by
two expressways and a major street.

Office areas are oriented towards a series
of interior courtyards, which are extensively
landscaped.

Headquarters of the General Electric Company
Fairfield, Connecticut

General Electric's headquarters was built for 850 employees in two buildings on a 100-acre site in suburban Fairfield, Connecticut. Completed in 1974, the 851,224-square-foot complex is situated at the top of a slope rising steeply from the bordering Merritt Parkway. A primary consideration in siting the buildings was to reduce the visual impact on the neighboring residential area. This was accomplished by limiting the height to three floors above grade, dividing 470,000 square feet of office space into two structures conforming to the land contours, and locating the parking for 722 cars in connected concrete podia beneath the structures.

The main entrance is approached from a formal court between the podia, which are clad in precast concrete panels with a warm tone granite aggregate finish. Above, exposed steel trusses span 81 feet to form the main office structure. The fine detailing and smooth white paint of the trusses contrast with the rough surface below. Recessing the tinted thermal glazing emphasizes the depth of the 6 ½-foot trusses. The resulting sheltered terraces shade the interior and facilitate maintenance of the window wall. Air handling units above the exterior steel spandrels are connected to condenser-compressor units on the roof.

SOM conducted space planning studies and developed a new concept for the distribution of private and pool space. Both buildings are organized around interior courts to maximize the perimeter area needed for private offices. Interior work areas share the advantages of exterior offices with regard to size, lighting, and flexibility. Special furniture was designed to meet diverse requirements and accommodate an anticipated need for future departmental expansion or contraction.

Site plan.

The complex is situated at the top of a steeply ▷ rising slope.

300'

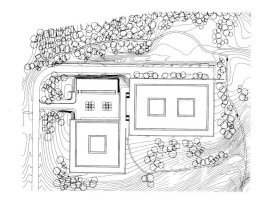

Plan (1st floor).

The long-span exterior steel structure was ▷
prefabricated. The fine detailing and smooth
white paint of the trusses contrast with the
textured surfaces below.

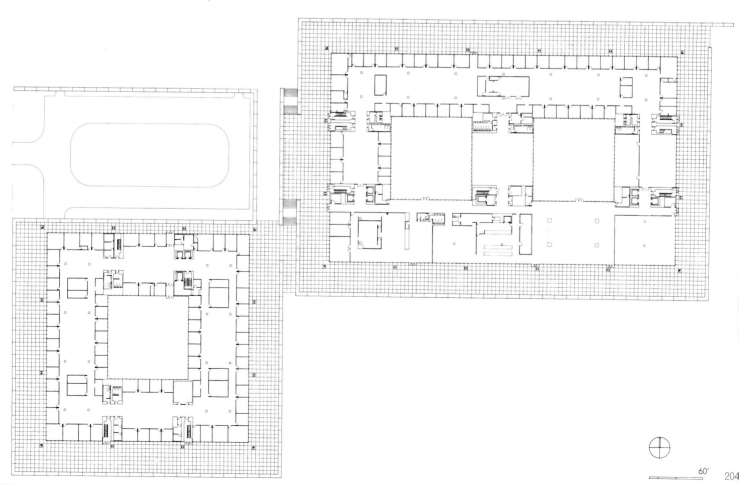

60'

Sixty State Street
Boston, Massachusetts

Located on an historically significant site in an area famed in America's past, the 38-story structure completed in 1978 was developed to provide over 800,000 square feet of premium rentable office and commercial retail space to the surrounding financial community. The design evolved an unusual shape on a setback location in order to lessen its high-rise impact on the quaint atmosphere of surrounding buildings and market areas.

Over 60 percent of the site has been developed for pedestrian use, highlighted by an elevated, landscaped terrace overlooking the surrounding historical area. Open plazas replace alleys and further encourage pedestrian traffic along celebrated walkways and the surrounding city streets.

The tower has a distinctive, eleven-sided configuration influenced in part by the irregular shape of the site. The building's angular shape restores the visual line between Old State House and Faneuil Hall, the city's two most important landmarks, which had been obstructed by buildings previously occupying the site. The unusual floor plan also results in highly desirable office space, offering a potential for nine outside corner offices on each floor and a variety of unobstructed views of the harbor and surrounding cityscape. There are 31 office floors averaging 22,500 square feet each, as well as five smaller penthouse floors defined by a multi-tiered sloping roof. Three levels of underground parking accommodate 200 cars.

The all-steel structural system consists of an exterior folded tube frame with moment-connected exterior columns spaced 10 feet on center, interconnected by deep spandrel beams which provide lateral load resistance for the tower. The steel columns are clad with Napoleon red granite set on triangular-shaped prefabricated steel strongbacks, between which are granite-clad spandrels and highly efficient dual-pane reflective tinted glass. The reddish gray tone of the granite was chosen for its compatibility with the traditional red brick and old granite used throughout the area.

Plans for The Bay Club, a private luncheon club, were integrated into the design of the building, located on the 33rd and 34th floors. A two-story wall of glass and a terraced seating arrangement afford a spectacular view of the harbor from every table.

General view from the southwest.

Napoleon red granite was chosen for compati- ▷ bility with the traditional red brick and granite used throughout the area.

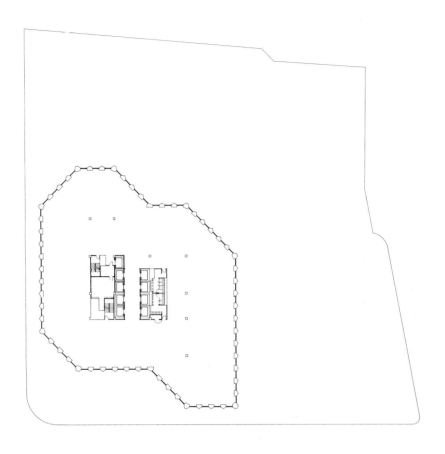

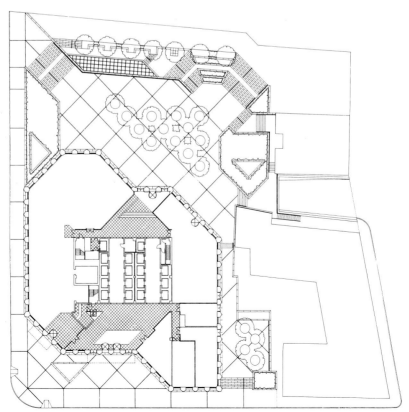

30'

◁ Plans (ground level, typical floor).

The angular shape of the building helps to restore the visual connection between the Old State House and Faneuil Hall, the city's two most important landmarks.

Harvard Square Station
Cambridge, Massachusetts

As the first element in a four-mile "Red Line" rail transit extension program, the Harvard Square Station project included the design, demolition, and reconstruction of a grim, aging 1912 rail transit station as well as the even older, physically integrated bus transfer facility located within Harvard Square's street system.

A significant design factor of the project was the mandate by the City of Cambridge to provide continuous bus and rail transit service throughout the five-year construction period, while also providing continuous vehicular and pedestrian flows to the university and adjacent business establishments.

An intensive community participation program throughout design and construction has assured that transit service and traffic have been maintained and that the numerous, sometimes conflicting, interests of the Harvard Square area were heard and included in the design.

Principal architectural objectives of the surface restoration include a significant increase in attractive pedestrian areas by creating three major landscaped plazas, the extensive use of shrubs, ground cover, planters, benches, and brick crosswalks to improve the pedestrian quality of the Square and to control vehicular flows. The vaulted 1928 Harvard Square kiosk was restored as the Square's central newsstand. A new, low, glazed structure provides entry to the station's mezzanine.

Principal architectural features of the subway station include the use throughout of strong curvilinear forms deriving from bus and rail tunnel geometry; clear expressions of roof structure spanning the radial geometry of the station's spaces; the strict integration of station lighting into the roof structure to further reinforce the powerful, curving geometry; and the use of elegant but low-maintenance interior finishes. These include tiled wall surfaces with stainless steel enclosing columns and other structural elements. Textured brick and granite pavers cover all floor surfaces, also patterned to reinforce the station's curved spaces.

Location map of the Boston-Cambridge metropolitan area.
1 Harvard Square Station

Views of platform level.

Train level (model). The station project includes ▷ the extension of an underground bus transfer facility. The sinuous forms of the station's spaces are derived from the required geometries of the merging bus and rail tunnels.

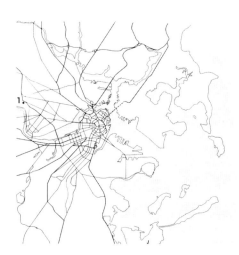

2

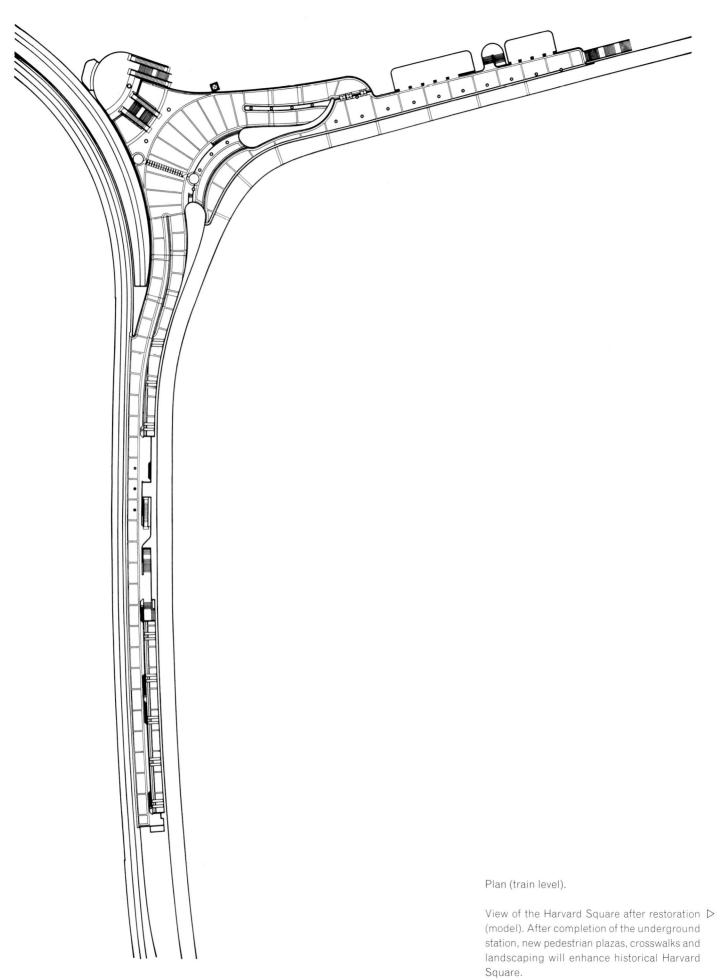

Plan (train level).

View of the Harvard Square after restoration ▷
(model). After completion of the underground
station, new pedestrian plazas, crosswalks and
landscaping will enhance historical Harvard
Square.

Reorganization of The Mall
Washington, D.C.

In preparation for the 1976 Bicentennial celebration, the National Park Service commissioned Skidmore, Owings & Merrill to develop a circulation plan for the Washington Mall, based on the firm's master plan for the area completed ten years earlier. In order to limit automobile traffic in this great park, two streets which had flanked the central greensward, Washington and Adams Drives, were replaced with pedestrian walks, and the central axis of the Washington Mall was restored. The importance of the disciplines of simplicity and restraint were emphasized throughout the design of this site, which lies at the heart of America's national iconography.

The guiding philosophy of the design was to retain the appropriate dignity of the Mall while encouraging an increased level of visitor activity. Four major pathways were established, two bordering the central lawn and two under the existing elm plantations, extending for nearly a mile between the Capitol Reflecting Pool and the Washington Monument.

Compacted crushed stone was chosen as the walkway material because of the simple scale afforded by its even and jointless texture. The design acknowledges the use of this material in many formal applications in France, whose rich landscape tradition influenced not only Pierre L'Enfant, Washington's original planner, but the celebrated Senate Park Commission of 1901 as well. Samples from Versailles, the Tuileries, and the Bois de Boulogne were procured and tests conducted to achieve the installed walkways.

The street furniture is carefully organized under the canopy of the mature elm plantations to discreetly reinforce the formal edges while deferring to the grand axial views. Special care was taken to protect the shallow roots of the vulnerable existing elm trees that flank the walks adjacent to the national museums. The benches and light standards were chosen to reiterate traditional elements, and both were constructed anew with castings made for the head and base of the historic "Olmsted" light standard, relamped to extend the Mall's use into the evening hours. A special paint color, "Capital Brown," was specifically developed for all metal surfaces of the project. Traditional park information kiosks were provided near the entrances to the national museums, and new trash receptacles, bicycle racks and drinking fountains were also located throughout the area.

A second phase of the award-winning design, as yet unbuilt, includes the narrowing and decorative repaving of two streets adjacent to the national museums as well. At some future date, these streets may be reserved for tourmobiles and bicycles, thereby completing the effort to remove the automobile from this foremost National Park.

Location plan.
1 Washington Mall
2 Constitution Gardens

View of the Mall towards the Washington ▷ Monument.

2

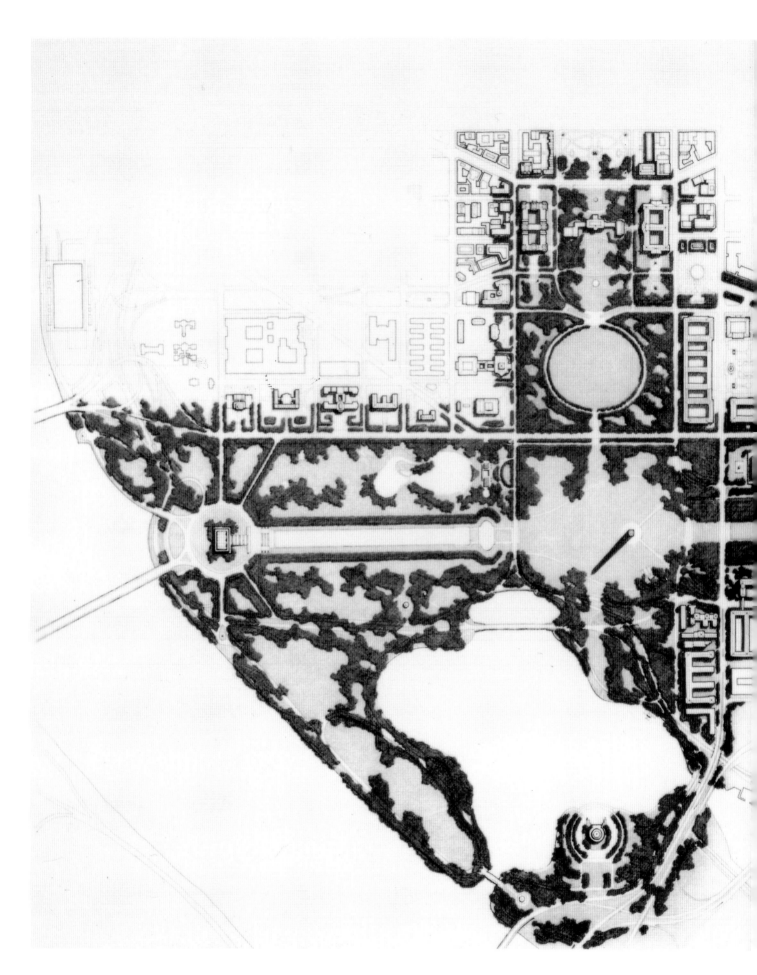

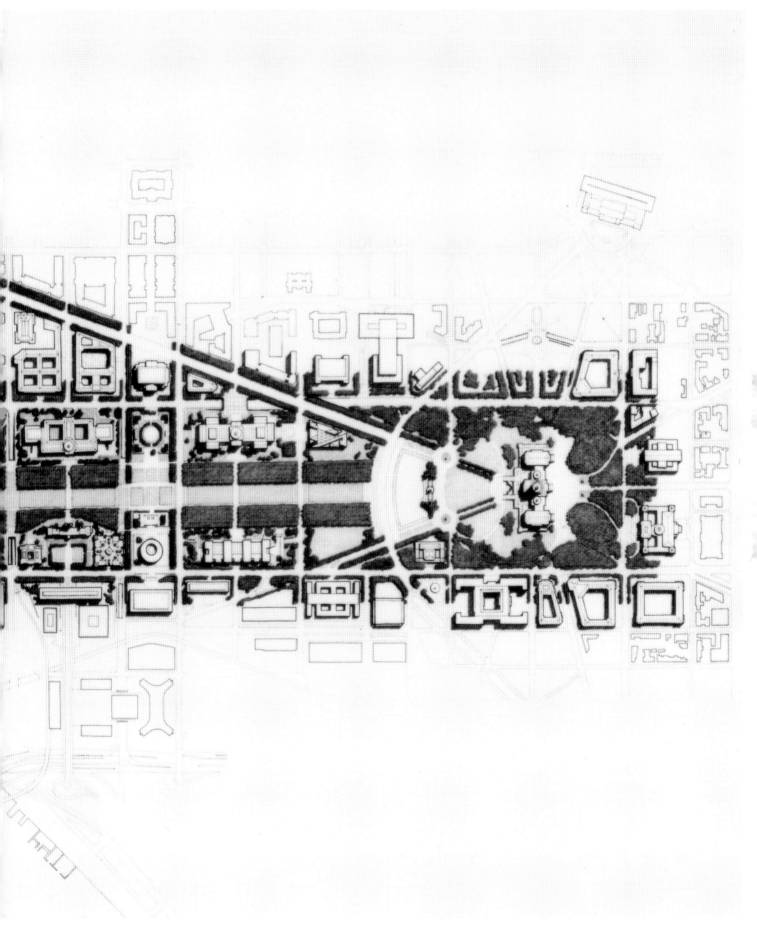

Views of the Mall towards the Capitol.

View of the Mall towards the Washington
Monument.

Constitution Gardens
Washington, D.C.

Constitution Gardens, completed in 1976, carries forward the goal of the National Park Service to reclaim the Washington Mall in the heart of the nation's capital as a pedestrian-oriented urban park. While the eastern half of the Mall was being constructed, Skidmore, Owings & Merrill's attention was again turned to the western half – a treeless site between Constitution Avenue and the Lincoln Memorial Reflecting Pool, occupied only by Navy Department buildings which had been constructed fifty years earlier to "temporarily" house World War I personnel.

After the removal of these barracks-like structures, an informal wooded park was developed on the 52-acre site. In keeping with the character of the rest of West Potomac Park surrounding the Lincoln Memorial, Constitution Gardens provides an urban oasis, sheltering pedestrians, tourists, and bicyclists from the heavy traffic of Constitution Avenue. A floor plane of softly contoured meadows is shaded by a canopy of trees as it slopes gently to meet the curving shoreline of an irregularly shaped, six-acre lake. A network of paths meanders in the shade following the contour lines. The design, deliberately executed as a "stage" for future activities, features paths which open into tree-encircled areas, providing a natural setting for modest garden structures and a variety of events. The site has been chosen as the appropriate setting for two new memorials, with the Vietnam Veterans Memorial located on the west in a meadowed area, and the Memorial to the 56 Signers of the Declaration of Independence on an island in the center of the lake.

The same sturdy Dutch elms that line the Reflecting Pool border the park on the south. From inside the park, the visitor can catch glimpses of the Washington Monument and the Smithsonian Institution buildings to the east and of the Lincoln Memorial to the west. Special care in both grading and the selection of plant materials was taken by SOM's architects and landscape designers, with Arnold Associates as consultant. Maple, beech, oak, gum, and tulip trees predominate, and graceful willows characterize the lake's central island, reached by a footbridge leading from the shore. At the eastern end of Constitution Gardens, a natural plaza on one of the highest points will be the future site of a visitor's pavilion, offering information, rest and refreshment facilities, and featuring tables along the terraces which step down to the water's edge.

Location plan.
1 Washington Mall
2 Constitution Gardens

Aerial view of the Constitution Gardens towards ▷
the Lincoln Memorial.

An undulating, informal and almost romantic landscape was created. Softly contoured meadows slope gently to meet the curving shoreline of an irregularly shaped lake.

Kuwait Chancery
Washington, D.C.

The Kuwait Chancery in Washington, located at the International Center, was completed in 1982. The building provides office space for 68 employees on three floors, including offices for cultural, military and educational activities. A 50-seat auditorium with audio-visual capabilities, a catering kitchen, guest restroom facilities, and an apartment for the resident engineer are in the first basement. Parking is available for 43 cars, 39 below grade and 4 on grade; a ramp from a loop road provides access to the garage and a covered off-street loading berth.

The two upper floors are supported by steel trusses cantilevering from two structural steel cores anchored at opposing corners. Suspended clear frameless glazing is used to enclose the entrance level. The second and third levels are glazed with insulating green-tinted frameless glass and spandrel panels with interior aluminum mullions. The building exterior is clad with stainless steel panels. Gray granite covers terrace and subgrade walls and the interior and exterior entrance level pavement.

In strong contrast to the smooth, high polish of the Chancery exterior, the interior is a colorful, highly decorative, vibrant space. The rotated square concept common to Islamic design is used to generate both building form and interior decorative motifs. A faceted skylight above the main reception hall refracts light with a prismatic effect across brightly painted walls. Enhancing the filtration of light, open wooden screens partition the ground floor space. Colorful marbles intricately inlaid in a geometric pattern contrast with gray granite paving. A rotated square fountain is the central decorative element of this space. Visitors and employees enjoy wide views of the surrounding area through expansive glass walls.

Plan (ground level).

Night view of the building. ▷

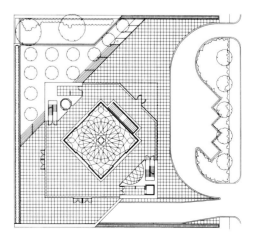

Section.

View of the interior courtyard. A faceted ▷
skylight refracts light with a prismatic effect
across brightly painted walls. Colorful marbles
intricately inlaid in a geometric pattern
contrast with gray granite paving.

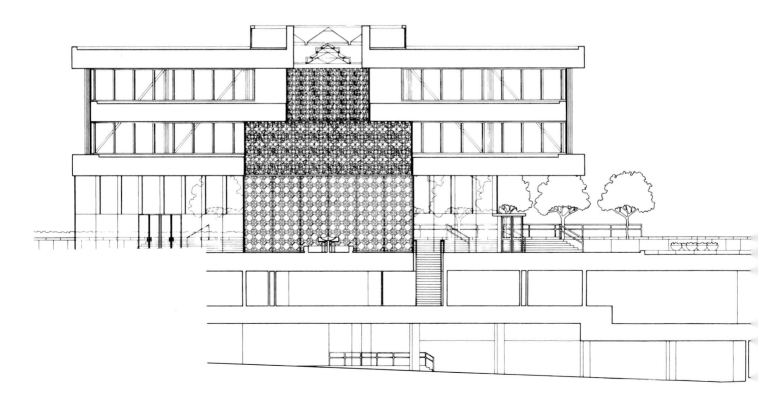

Georgia-Pacific Center
Atlanta, Georgia

The Georgia-Pacific Corporation world headquarters in downtown Atlanta was completed in 1982. At 52 stories, the 1,360,000-square-foot tower is one of the largest and tallest buildings in the southeastern United States. Georgia-Pacific Center rises above a landscaped plaza at the intersection of Peachtree and Houston Streets, and borders Margaret Mitchell Square.

The building fills its site to respect the openness of the square. Its stepped profile is a design response to the site and the varied heights of surrounding buildings. Another major design response occurs in plan, with the west facade set at a 60-degree angle in order to relate the tower to the intersection of the major streets. The stepped profile is also a way of combining the economic advantages of a conventional elevator system with the range of smaller floor areas required by the Atlanta market. A range of floor sizes was desired, from about 28,000 square feet for Georgia-Pacific's floors in the lower portion of the building to 24,000 square feet, 20,000 square feet and 17,000 square feet for tenant floors in the upper portions.

Structurally, the building is a modified tube with columns closely spaced at 10-foot intervals around the perimeter. Three sides are connected by stiff spandrel beams and completed by a truss on the east wall. A 7-foot-square window is placed in each 10-foot bay. The perimeter tube and the core act together through connecting floor members to resist wind stresses.

Mechanical equipment rooms with direct access to outside air are located on each floor. The air/water system has variable air volume for interior space and a fan coil system for the perimeter. The energy-efficient lighting system is based on the building's 5-foot-by-5-foot planning module. The fixture itself delivers task levels of lighting only in task areas, with reduced or ambient levels in circulation, reception or lounge areas.

The Georgia-Pacific Center includes a low-rise building for a computer center, 250-seat auditorium, conference rooms, a restaurant, a cafeteria, and shops. A health club and jogging track are located on the roof of the garage, which provides parking for more than 700 cars.

Section.

The building profile is a design response to the ▷ site and the varied heights of the surrounding buildings.

Plans (ground level, typical floor).

Elevation. ▷

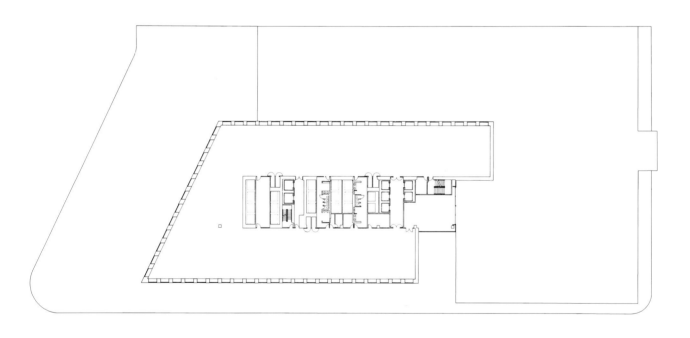

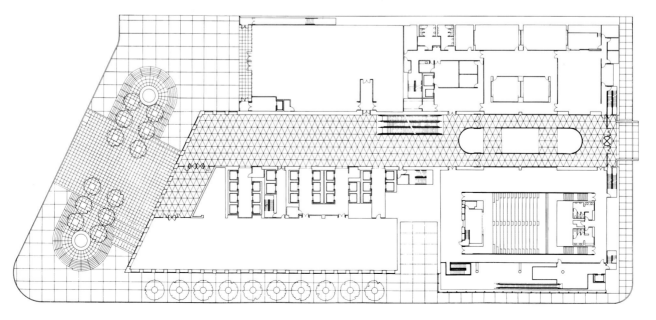

30'

23

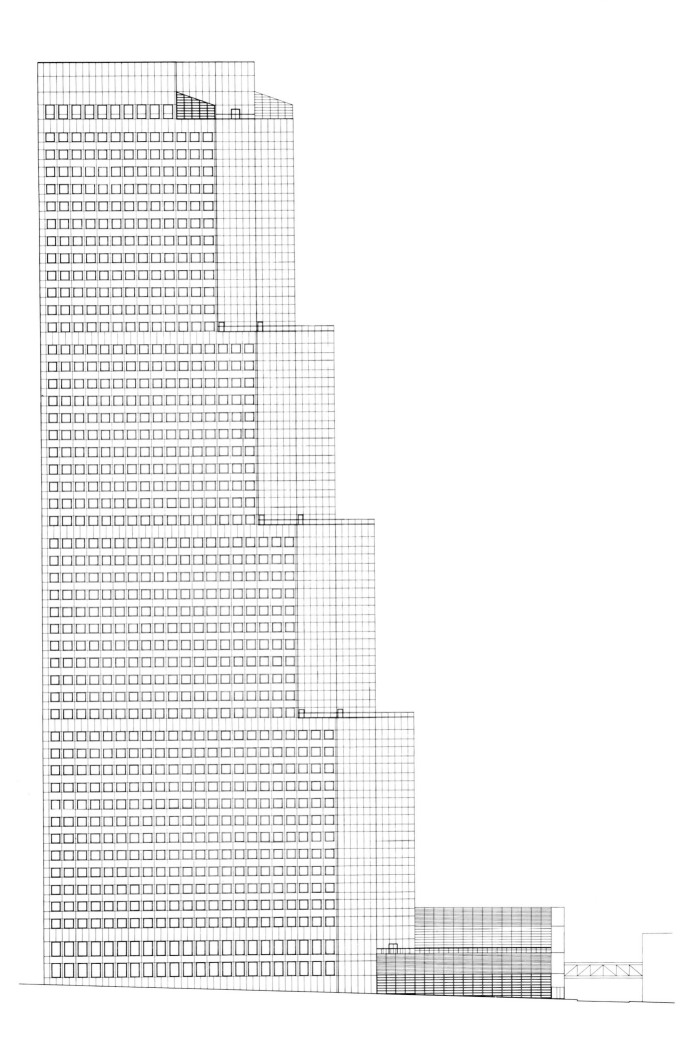

International

In the 1970's, as now, SOM won important architectural and urban design commissions on several continents where nations are undergoing rapid industrialization and urbanization. Each project stirred debate over modern architecture's quest for universality. Should architects propose universal, mechanistic forms, memorable for originality and modernity, or should they catch indigenous themes and native responses to climate and terrain? Did SOM resolve that debate in their marvelous Haj Terminal at Jeddah, Royal Dutch Shell Petroleum Company Headquarters in The Hague [2], or the U.S. Embassy in Moscow [3]? In a decade when the 1973 oil crisis provoked doubts about energy-dependent environment, SOM sent young designers to preindustrial nations where neither building technologies nor social patterns were familiar. Their plans for Helwan University, south of Cairo [4], and Kebangsaan University in Sabah, East Malaysia [5, 6], reveal their efforts at evolving form from native technologies. In contrast to the urbane continental client who wanted a modern, art-filled Parisian office and won SOM's most elegant Park Avenue response, governmental leaders in economically ascendant nations often worried whether Western aesthetics and technology would disrupt traditional social and cultural patterns. SOM's earlier Banque Lambert [7] was wonderful for Brussels, but Egypt, Iran and Malaysia had neither the technology nor corporate structure ready for it.

SOM was by no means united on the question of architecture for developing nations. Proposed forms ranged from expressions of indigenous themes to declarations of bold inventions. For the Banco de Occidente buildings in Guatemala City [8], SOM/Chicago partners Bruce Graham and Adrian Smith modelled light, color and texture within gently scaled spaces and elemental, vernacular forms reminiscent of Luis Barragan. In contrast, the National Commercial Bank of Jeddah [9], proposed by SOM/New York partner Gordon Bunshaft, is a tall triangular prism pierced by a central well and courtyards. However much the prismatic frame may reduce glare and dissipate heat, it is original, and its abutting circular garage and adjoining banking hall lack Islamic or Saudi reference. Is such new universal configuration wanted, and does it announce Saudi Arabia's emancipation, or only private ambitions that may be transitory?

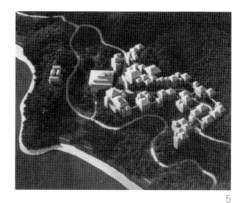

1 Skyline of Jeddah, Saudi Arabia.
2 Addition to the headquarters of Royal Dutch Shell, The Hague, The Netherlands.
3 United States Embassy, Moscow, USSR.
4 Helwan University, Helwan, Egypt.
5,6 Kebangsaan University, Sabah, East Malaysia.
7 Banque Lambert, Brussels, Belgium.

8

10

8 Montufar branch of the Banco de Occidente, Guatemala City, Guatemala.
9 National Commercial Bank, Jeddah, Saudi Arabia.
10 Kuwait Markets Group – Ahmed Al Jaber Street Commercial Center, Kuwait City, Kuwait.
11 Headquarters of the Grupo Industrial Alfa, Monterrey, Mexico.
12 First Canadian Centre, Calgary, Canada.

It can of course be argued that such an avowedly modern, universal form is desirable. If an agrarian or nomadic nation strikes riches and overnight acquires airplanes, microwave antennas, telephones, televisions, computers, and modern medicine, why should it not celebrate its arrival and ascendancy in original symbols? If they are exquisite, even daring and brilliant, they may set goals and summon pride. Then, too, some aspiring nations may be more ready than others to import both social change and an architecture that hastens the change. Moreover, there is nothing local about the modern international financial corporation. The commercial corporation is universal, and, with innovative, distinctive forms, SOM/New York partner Michael McCarthy conveys that message in the Al Jaber Commercial Complex [10] for his Kuwaiti clients. A similar message is sent by SOM's Mexican and Canadian projects. For the Grupo Alfa in Mexico, SOM proposed vaulted halls and internal gardens for its headquarters south of Monterrey [11]. Acknowledging the Energy Belt alliance in western Canada, SOM/New York's First Canadian Centre in Calgary [12] consists of two tall towers joined by a triangular three-story pavilion for the Bank of Montreal.

What messages in a foreign culture should be heard? If Riyadh has only remnants of a mud brick fort and the Bedouin has no heritage of permanent architecture, should architects invent modern forms for Saudi Arabia or spring variations on Jeddah's Victorian villas and Beaux Arts banks, capture themes from Spain's Islamic architecture and recall Berber villages in North Africa or mosques in Iran? Or will it suffice to design Western structures and add local crafts and ornament, like the batik banners suspended within SOM's otherwise universal Lanka Oberoi hotel lobby in Sri Lanka [13]? Downtown Casablanca and Beirut sadly show the result of feckless modernism. Deciding that such insensitivities are intolerable, SOM's partners sought for more.

Where SOM met regional challenges was in North Africa and the Middle East. There, clients often needed help in organizing the programs for hospitals and universities. SOM/Chicago partner Walter Netsch encouraged the Algerian Ministry of Higher Education and Scientific Research to retain American educational consultants. The resulting University of Tizi-Ouzou [14, 15] arranges technical disciplines around four courtyards, each offering specialized libraries, classrooms and laboratories.

11

12

9

13

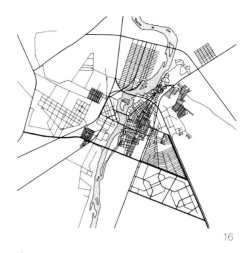

16

17

A second Algerian campus, the University of Blida, assigns fifteen fields of study to four specialized colleges, with university-owned student housing and a separate site for Blida's Teaching Hospital.

For Helwan University in Egypt, SOM/Chicago's Netsch and DeStefano developed sequences of courtyard and building that reflect a set of principles SOM had developed. Foremost was the goal of solving each project's problem in its broadest urban implications. A second was to combine residential space with work places in culturally relevant ways. A third was to find means to reduce dependency on electricity and emphasize natural means for modifying temperature and gaining ventilation. A fourth principle was to use local materials and manpower and modularize mass-produced units so that labor-intensive, nonmechanized societies could assemble them. The fifth was to recognize privacies and celebrate any special reverences for water, shade and canopy, and the sixth was to enrich public ways and sanctuaries.

Those six principles guided SOM's town planning in the Middle East's desert regions where governments started new towns to support petrochemical plants and ports. Occupying flat, treeless sites and threatened by scarce water, flash floods, and searing winds, such towns feel the sun's heat, which divides each day into work and school at dawn, middays at home, late afternoons at work and evenings at public leisure, with further intervals marked by frequent religious worship. Those features of time, climate, terrain and culture emerged in SOM's discussions at Shiraz in 1975 when SOM partners Goldstein, DeStefano and Khan joined Teheran's Mandala Collaborative in planning important Iranian towns.

In Iran's Khuzestan, the oil-rich province where five great rivers converge and flow into the Persian Gulf, SOM/San Francisco planned a new perimetal community, Jondi Shapour [16, 17], whose master plan in 1976 was endorsed as a model for Iranian government-sponsored housing. SOM/San Francisco, later augmented by SOM/Chicago, also planned a new town on a flat plain near Bandar Shapour [18, 19]. Selecting a site distant from Bandar Shapour's refineries and petrochemical industries, the urban designers proposed a lake and reservoir and brought precious water in open irrigation canals along the major boulevard and subsidiary roads within urban districts. Paths radiating from the bazaar lead to nodes and intersections, which are the principal

14

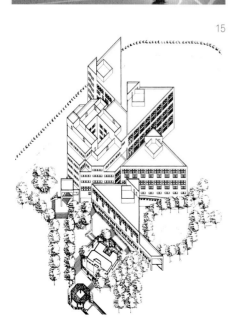

15

18

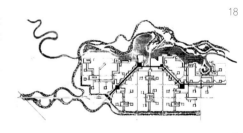

19

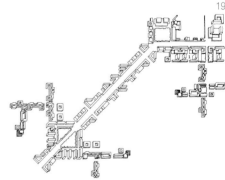

13 Lanka Oberoi Hotel, Colombo, Sri Lanka.
14,15 University of Tizi-Ouzou, Tizi-Ouzou, Algeria.
16,17 Jondi Shapour New Town, Jondi Shapour, Iran.
18,19 Bandar Shapour New Town, Bandar Shapour, Iran.

23

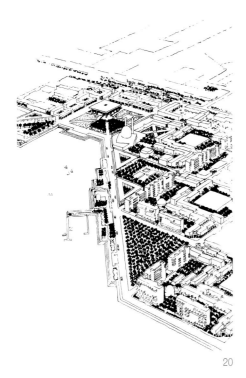

20

locations for religious, medical, educational and governmental buildings.

SOM's work in the Middle East culminated in large planning projects in Saudi Arabia. For the new petrochemical town on the Red Sea south of Yanbu [20], SOM/San Francisco laid an orthogonal grid on the port's curved shoreline and assigned a triangular site to the town center. For Umm Al-Qura University, formerly called the King Abdul Aziz University, near Makkah [21], SOM/Chicago, led by partners Roger Seitz and Fazlur Khan, proposed a campus that embodies many features of the historic Islamic "madrassa." While neither Yanbu's new town nor the university will be built to SOM's plans, the most important of SOM's Saudi Arabian projects, the Haj Terminal at Jeddah [22], was completed and has drawn international acclaim. Initially, the Haj Terminal project was undertaken by SOM/New York partner Gordon Wildermuth, who had led the team designing the Jeddah Airport since 1975. Soon, however, the Haj Terminal enlisted Gordon Bunshaft, Raul de Armas, Roy Allen and John Winkler in New York and then engaged Chicago's Fazlur Khan and Parambir Gujral, who probed structure and energy in membrane and tensile structures. It is a remarkable feat of collaboration and advanced SOM's interoffice strength.

A tented city in the desert, the Haj Terminal is an ancient symbol, the gateway to Islam, achieved by modern artistry. It was imagined by architects who did not withhold their best efforts at wedding technology to aesthetic insight. Neither a universal modernism nor a local traditionalism, the Haj Terminal proves that modern technology may have magnificent integrity while serving indigenous cultural themes.

21

22

20 Yanbu New Town, Yanbu, Saudi Arabia.
21 King Abdul Aziz University, Makkah, Saudi Arabia.
22 Haj Terminal, King Abdul Aziz International Airport, Jeddah, Saudi Arabia.

Headquarters of the Banco de Occidente
Guatemala City, Guatemala

In 1978 three buildings were completed in Guatemala City for Banco de Occidente, one of the oldest banking institutions in Guatemala: the three-story headquarters in the ancient city center and two smaller suburban branch banks. Architectural continuity was sought for all locations through the use of indigenous colors, similar effects of light and shadow, and repetitive use of textures and materials. In contrast to the typical approach to local reconstruction projects, the architects consciously reinforced the buildings' relationship to the Guatemalan context by using only locally available construction materials and adopting local architectural concepts, such as open court-yards, terraces, gardens, fountains and trellises. Because of frequent local power failures, the buildings are designed to function without artificial illumination. Heating and cooling systems are omitted from the buildings, and all three poured-in-place reinforced concrete structures are designed to resist Zone 3 earthquake forces.

The headquarters provides maximum teller and public contact areas on level 1; executive offices, board room and semi-public contact on level 2; and an employee lounge and non-public functions at level 3. Major design elements are exterior walls predominantly of opaque stucco, an interior/exterior courtyard, and a two-story banking room with a translucent fabric roof to allow soft natural light to enter the hall. A stone base at street level provides a durable surface to withstand high pedestrian traffic and vandalism. Terrace openings to the north and setback openings on the west control light, and operable wood louvers modulate ventilation.

Plan (ground floor).

Interior views. ▷

Pages 240–241:
Exterior views.

View of the courtyard.

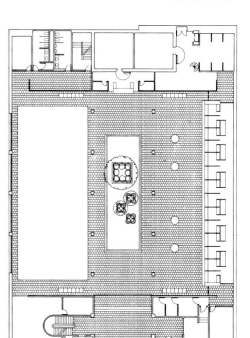

30'

Montufar Branch of the Banco de Occidente
Guatemala City, Guatemala

The 4,500-square-foot Montufar branch is a small, eight-teller facility located on property with existing party walls on all sides. The facility is accessible from two points through existing shopping centers. Skylights were designed to provide natural light and ventilation with minimal direct sunlight on work surfaces. Each skylight uses concrete block louvers for ventilation. A large skylit courtyard with reflecting pool is used to increase the sense of openness and strengthen the illusion of interior as exterior space.

Plan (ground floor).

Skylights provide natural light and ventilation ▷ with minimal direct sunlight.

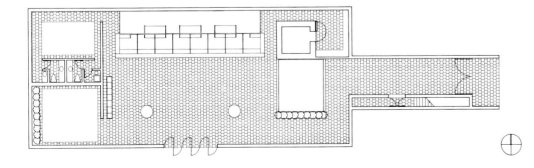

Indigenous colors and materials, combined with subtle effects of light and shadow, reinforce the building's relationship to the Guatemalan context.

First Canadian Centre
Calgary, Alberta, Canada

The 2,000,000-square-foot First Canadian Centre, under construction on an L-shaped site in downtown Calgary, is scheduled for completion in 1985. This complex will completely fill its 2.18-acre site, with a banking pavilion occupying the corner.

The banking pavilion, a soaring cathedral-like space, rises under uneven slopes to a 10-story peak. Inset between the towers, it is the complex's focal point, connecting three levels of public space. The completely glazed pavilion is a steel frame structure faced with white granite. From the cold outdoors, tenants and visitors enter a climate-controlled, light and airy hall warmed by red granite floors and walls.

The taller tower rises 64 stories, cutting back at the 42nd floor, while the shorter 43-story tower cuts back at the 22nd floor. At the lower levels, the plan is in the shape of a large parallelogram with truncated corners; the upper-level plan is halved at a 45-degree angle. This configuration produced varying floor sizes to suit the needs of both large and small companies. The interior spaces are designed for an open office plan and optimize perimeter space for private offices. Sloped, gray-tinted, insulated glass roofs double as exterior walls for the uppermost floors, creating three-dimensional spaces in the sky. These floors can be cut back to create a mezzanine level at four locations within the towers. Below grade space contains two levels of parking for 165 cars and loading facilities.

The structural system for the towers is based on a tube-in-tube concept involving an exterior reinforced concrete-framed tube and an interior shear wall core tube. The 64-story tower is a composite concrete tube-in-tube system with a long-span steel truss floor system, while the 43-story tower is an all-concrete system. The exterior column spacing for the 43-story tower was modified to make the tube grid more responsive to table form construction for the concrete floors.

The pre-assembled cladding system for the towers consolidates in one pre-cast concrete sandwich panel the white Sardinian polished granite finish material (with joints sealed), building insulation, metal flashing, window frames, slightly reflective silvery blue window glazing, and window-cleaning tracks.

General view (photomontage).

Plans (ground level, typical floor). ▷

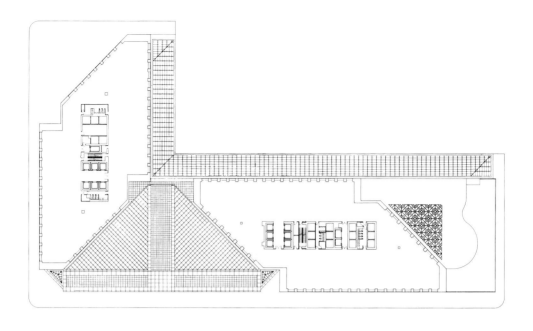

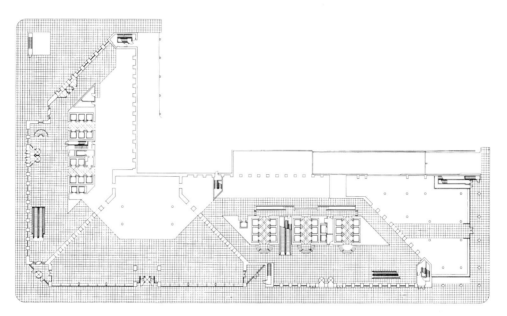

30'

Agnelli Suite
Paris, France

This executive suite, completed in 1976, occupies the top floor of the 44-story Tour Fiat office tower in the La Défense section of Paris.

Colors and materials for this 7,400-square-foot interiors project were selected to complement an existing private art collection. Travertine walls and floors of the main reception gallery are punctuated by polished stainless steel covering doors and columns. The gallery is reached by a round private elevator from the floor below. Two large offices, a conference room, a board room, and secretarial space are located on one side of the gallery. Partitions separate these rooms from the main gallery, allowing perimeter circulation. On the opposite side of the gallery are a dining room, kitchen, bedroom, bath, and sauna, in addition to small support offices. In the dining room, leather and stainless steel chairs surround a stainless steel and glass dining table. The two large private offices are furnished with desks of English oak burl and stainless steel, and leather and stainless steel chairs. The couches are upholstered with handwoven materials and handwoven light wool rugs cover teak floors. Lacquered wood sunscreens open to reveal sweeping views over the city.

Plan.

Executive dining room. ▷

30'

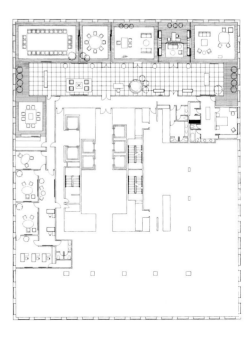

250

In the reception gallery travertine walls and floors are contrasted by polished stainless steel, covering doors and columns.

Addition to the Headquarters of Royal Dutch Shell
The Hague, The Netherlands

Scheduled to begin construction in 1983, the new central office building for the Shell Petroleum Company will contain approximately 300,000 square feet of space on an 86,000 square-foot site adjacent to the existing headquarters in The Hague. The surrounding context consists of three- to-four-story residential blocks, a prominent point across from the site being occupied by a three-story office building designed by the Dutch architect Berlage during the 20's. Height limitations for the site have been established by the authorities with the intention of safeguarding the predominately low-rise residential character of the area.

In keeping with European traditions the client provided program requirements for office space consisting of typically small offices, each with a window for natural light, and offices for the managing directors with associated meeting and dining facilities. The old neighboring office building was to be integrated as a functioning part with the new additions while maintaining its significant historical image.

The program requirements for all offices to have natural light resulted in a design concept grouping office space around several interior courts. This continues the scheme of the old headquarters which has two open courts; however, the new solution provides for enclosed skylit atria. Adjacent to the old offices, the new headquarters building is a square, eight-story block with a major central atrium to which a four-story low-rise element with two atria is linked on the other side. The new structures are made to appear smaller than they really are by varied external massing and stepbacks. Responding to the neighborhood character, traditional brick will be used for the exterior, with granite cladding the first floor base to underline the horizontal impression of the new buildings.

Plan (ground floor) and elevation.

View of the new headquarters building from ▷ the north.

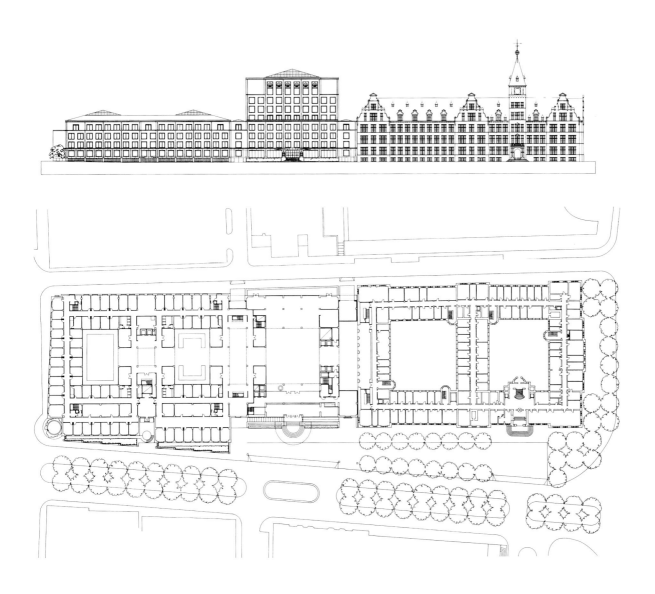

The main entry to the new headquarters is the left, adjacent to the existing headquarters.

View of entry atrium.

The stair in the upper atrium connects the executive floors.

United States Embassy
Moscow, USSR

On a site of 10.5 acres in metropolitan Moscow the proposed United States Embassy will provide 633,000 square feet of enclosed space with offices, service and community facilities as well as 146 staff apartments. The site is generally rectangular in shape but has a gentle slope to the west. The housing consists of three- and four-story terraces along the long east and west sides of the site, providing each unit with individual access and identity as well as with favorable morning and afternoon sun exposure. The housing thus serves as enclosures for a large central common – the focus and unifying space for the whole complex. Whereas the top surface of this green common is used for recreational and social activities, numerous service and community facilities including a gymnasium, theater, commissary and medical center, along with parking, are located below. There will be ample depth and strong enough structure to support extensive landscaping, including large trees.

Due to the natural slope of the site the lower-level facilities are accessible and obtain daylight at the western edge of the common. Located at the south end, the eight-story square office block bounds the common space. An equally square forecourt, the size of the building plan, will link the main entry to public access from Devyatinsky Avenue. At the opposite end of the common is the school, with its playground directed south towards the greensward and full sunlight. There will be a secondary entrance to the complex on this side.

The common in the center of the complex essentially is an outdoor living room for the whole community, with an unbroken surface of grass and large trees introduced in carefully placed groupings, shrubs lining the edges. The space is large enough for casual ball games at one end and for mothers walking or perambulating their babies simultaneously at the other end. At its east and west edges the common is bounded by wide walkways, the western one being at the lower level due to the natural slope of the site. Both of these walkways are sized to accept cars under special circumstances or at occasional emergencies – like moving household goods, service vehicles and guest parking in the evening.

Site plan.

Plans (lower level, street level, upper level).

Perspective view of the entire complex. ▷

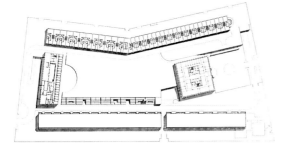

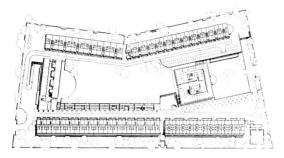

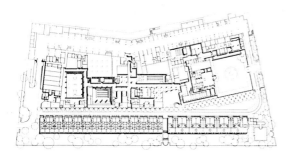

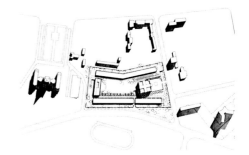

258

Teaching Hospital and Housing Communities at the University of Blida
Blida, Algeria

On a fanning alluvial plain at the foothills of the Atlas Mountains southwest of Algiers, the University of Blida will serve 10,000 students. The master plan for its teaching hospital, to be completed in 1986, is designed to permit shared use of services and equipment often duplicated in a departmentally organized hospital.

The core hospital consists of diagnostic and surgery blocks, outpatient clinics and bedcare units. Major medical services are located in the diagnostic block. Teaching departments are assigned to outpatient modules and sited directly opposite those diagnostic services to which they most relate. Bedcare units, located between the diagnostic and surgery blocks, have pedestrian bridges and ramps to both service areas.

The hospital will also include a service block, dental clinic and special care units. The service block, parallel to the diagnostic block, houses central linen and food services for the entire complex. The psychiatric and infectious disease wards, physically isolated from the core hospital, each include autonomous diagnostic and outpatient services.

Departmental disciplines are accommodated along double-loaded corridors in each leg of the outpatient modules. Central desks at the apex of each angle serve two corridors of physicians' offices and ECO rooms. Thirty-seat lecture halls linking two modules are used for advanced training in specialized fields. These lecture halls and the general classroom building are at the northern edge of the complex, adjacent to the main university campus.

Pinwheel bedcare units are designed to minimize staff and support space requirements. Bed units are arranged so as to segregate views into men's and women's wards. Small courtyards, formed by the building geometry, can be used as waiting areas for family members. The main entry court, formed by the angled diagnostic and surgery blocks, is also a terraced garden waiting area with small shops and tea rooms.

At the southern end of the 80-acre site, the infectious disease ward is fully isolated. Interior, uncontaminated staff circulation supplements the patient walkway system between bedcare units, diagnostic services and physicians' offices.

The diagonally sited buildings step down the modest slope of the site. To increase their seismic stability, each long block is designed as a series of small, structurally independent elements with expansion joints and exterior service towers. The teaching hospital complex, as the entire university, uses Algerian materials, in-situ concrete frames and masonry infill. Buildings' widths allow for cross ventilation with operable, wooden-frame windows.

The three housing communities, each for 2,000 students, were designed to encourage social interaction at a village scale. Each student suite consists of six double sleeping rooms of 100 square feet grouped around a central living room and sharing common toilet and shower rooms. Exterior entry stairs lead to shared covered balconies off the living areas. A concern for efficient ventilation and sunscreening resulted in the development of an octagonal module, formed by paired sleeping rooms, which became the basic design element.

Within the walled enclosure, each men's or women's community follows one of three basic configurations. Blocks containing student suites and common activity facilities are situated in response to individual site conditions, internal circulation patterns and social groupings. Further emphasizing the community sense at different scales, a hierarchy of outdoor spaces reaches from a central activity area to large landscaped courts and small courtyards among the housing clusters. Common activity centers are located near the main entrance to each community and differ from the housing clusters by their rectilinear geometry. They include a restaurant, library and multi-purpose auditorium, meeting and activity rooms, as well as an infirmary and shops.

In all communities, native materials such as locally fabricated wooden-frame operable windows and decorative tile sills will be used. The stucco facades will be painted in a variety of colors. SOM has also designed three student housing complexes for the university in Annaba, 300 miles further east. Three variations of the housing unit combined with several activity space arrangements give each 20-acre site a unique character.

Location map of Algeria.
1 Blida
2 Algiers
3 Tizi-Ouzo
4 Annaba
5 Mediterranean Sea
6 Atlantic Ocean

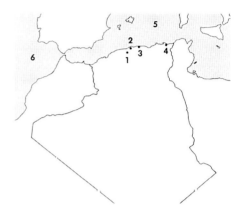

Site plan of the University of Blida.
A Academic departments and support facilities
B Housing community no. 1
C Teaching hospital
1 Academic pavilion
2 Outpatient services
3 Diagnostic block
4 Registration and main entry
5 Main courtyard
6 Bedcare units
7 Surgery block
8 Administration/dental block
9 Department head offices
10 Psychiatric ward
11 Service block
12 Infectious diseases

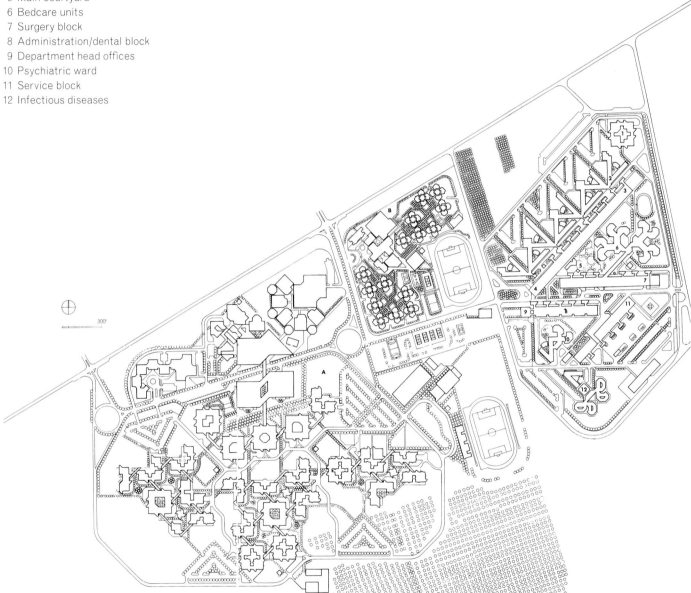

300'

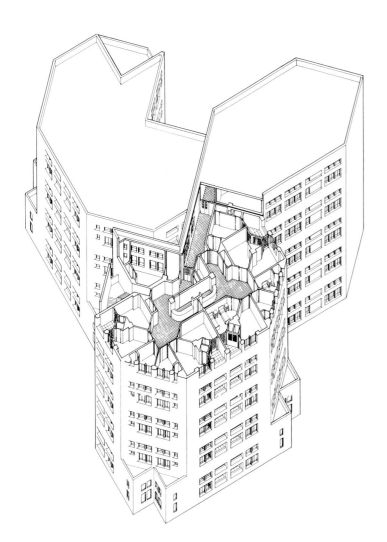

Axonometric view of a bedcare cluster.

Plan of a bedcare unit.

30'

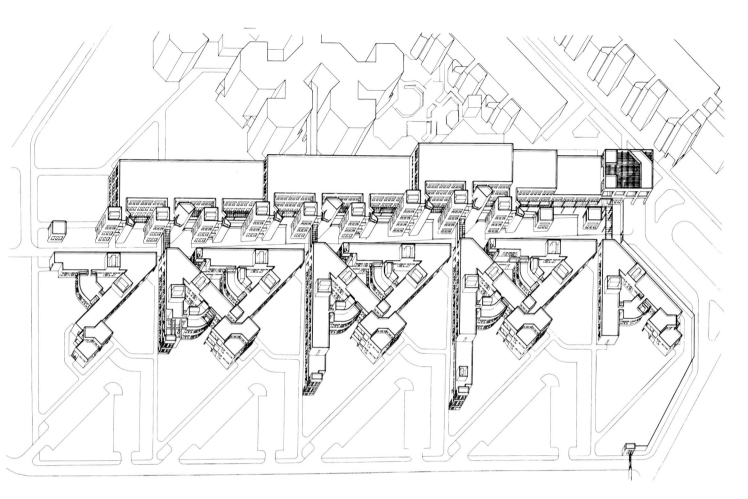

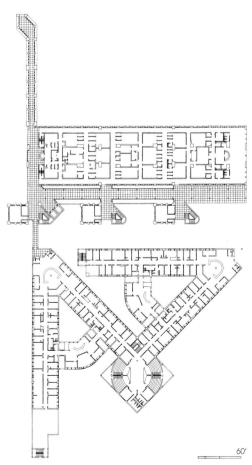

60'

Axonometric view of the diagnostic block and the outpatient services.

Partial plan (second floor) of the diagnostic block and the outpatient services.

View of an academic pavilion.

Axonometric view of a typical academic
pavilion.

Site plan of an academic department.

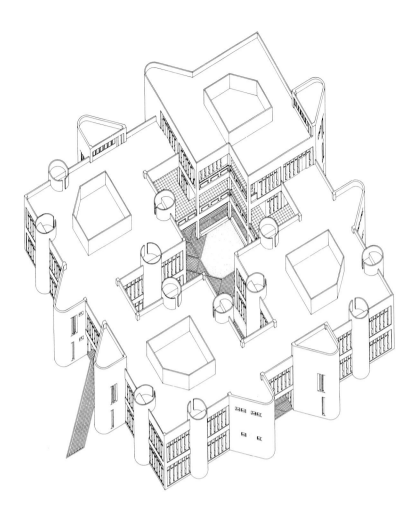

150'

King Abdul Aziz University
Makkah, Saudi Arabia

The proposed site for the university is in a relatively flat valley surrounded by low, barren mountains west of the Holy City of Makkah. Conceived as a meeting place for scholars throughout the Islamic world, the academic setting was designed to reflect the social, cultural and historical patterns of Saudi Arabian traditions. The overall development calls for a student population of 10,000 men and 5,000 women, with future expansion for an additional 50 percent.

The essential relationships of major campus components reflect a commitment to the traditional separation of male and female students. There are effectively two campuses. The internal relationships of each campus reflect similar principles of organization but, with the exception of administrative functions, each operates as a distinct entity. No allowance for either academic or social contact among students or faculty members of opposite sexes has been provided.

The Makkah-Jeddah Road separates the site into two distinct areas. All academic and administrative functions, single student residences, student services, and physical support facilities are located north of the road; also included are housing for married students and single and married faculty and staff. The site south of the Makkah-Jeddah Road will support a housing community containing 2,400 dwelling units and includes a number of commercial and service support facilities. In order to maintain traditional social values, the general form and texture of the communities is intended to incorporate characteristics of established Islamic urban settlements.

The master plan, completed in 1978, incorporates a low rise, high-density configuration of tightly clustered buildings. The desire for easy, comfortable pedestrian movement underlies the creation of spaces among buildings and limits distances between component elements, resulting in a compact overall geometry.

A building form using thermal mass was developed to respond to the extreme climatic conditions prevalent in Makkah. Housing units were designed to maximize night ventilation. Courtyard elements maximize air ventilation and add daylight to interior spaces. Coupled with the thermal mass, this produces free cooling for a substantial portion of the year.

Location plan of Makkah.
1 Existing university
2 New campus

Plan of the women's university. ▷

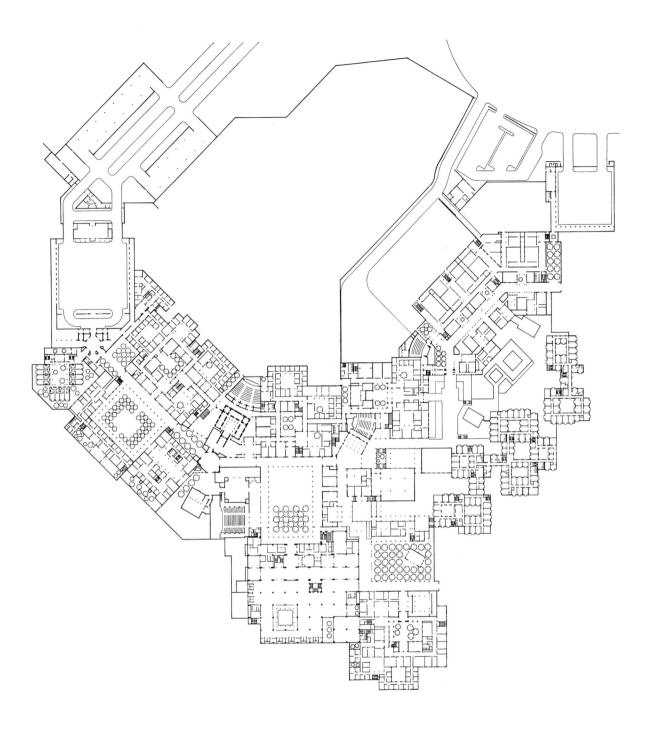

120'

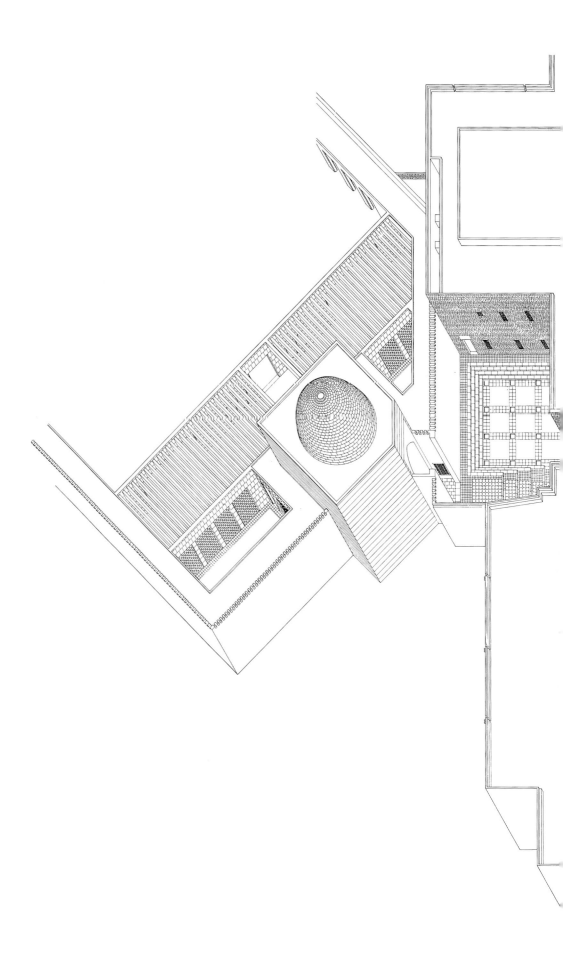

Axonometric view of a courtyard building in
the women's university.

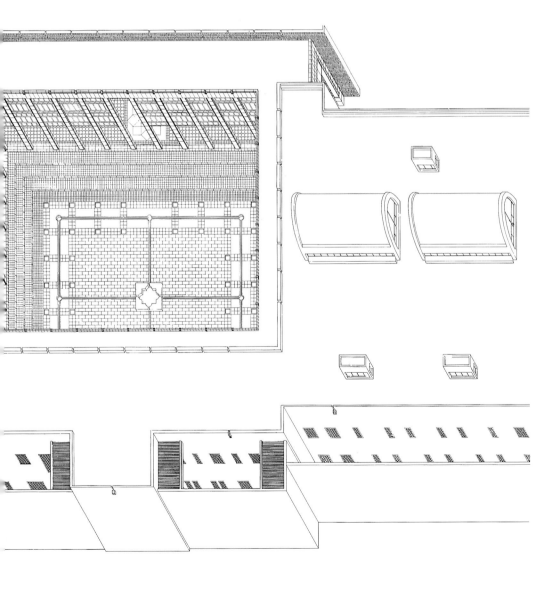

Section through a typical faculty court in the women's university.

Plan of the reception court in the women's university.

Courtyard portals in the women's university. ▷

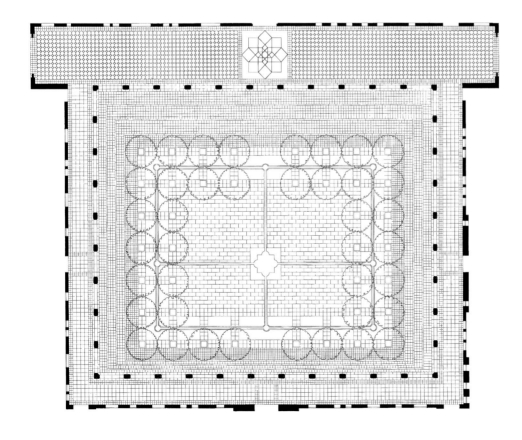

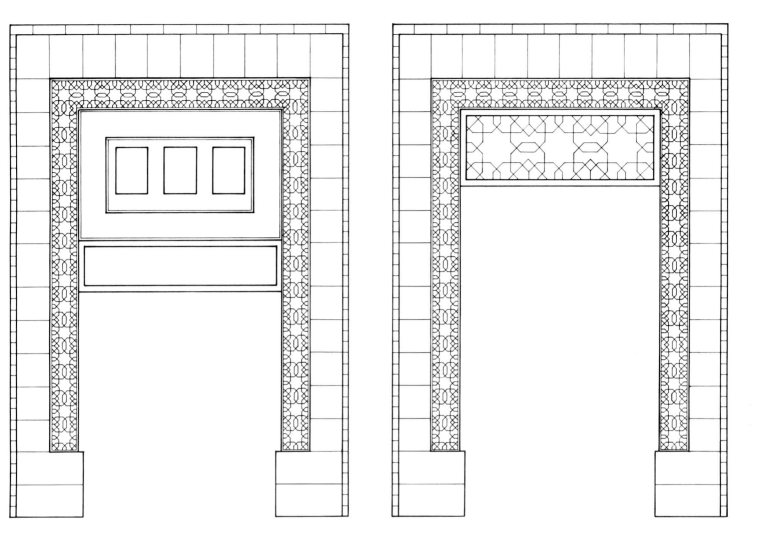

Yanbu New Town
Yanbu, Saudi Arabia

The SOM master plan for the New Town of Yanbu creates a strong framework that uses interchangeable modules and building prototypes. This framework permits program flexibility and change as well as insuring an impression of completeness at any point in the thirty-year construction period.

The new town is to be built on a 13,580-acre site on the Red Sea five miles south of the existing town of Yanbu. The primary employment base for the projected 150,000 population is petrochemical production and shipping.

Initial development is to occur blockwise from the town center with the first residential unit and the center being mutually supportive. Community social services are distributed throughout the town. By contrast, mosques, shops, health clinics and schools are clustered within residential neighborhoods.

The central planning concept provides a clearly defined physical framework which respects two overriding concerns. First, the climate of the region is extremely harsh and, second, the cultural heritage of future inhabitants will be unusually complex. People of widely ranging backgrounds must live side by side in a desert setting. The plan's major concepts are to respect multiple cultural backgrounds, promote privacy between residential units and provide protection from the desert sun. The physical design concept creates shade at every opportunity as well as privacy between neighborhood districts and individual buildings.

Residential areas are composed of modular housing types which include single-family units, villas, townhouses and walk-up apartments. The largest percentage of neighborhoods are developed at the lowest densities. The town center is the highest density area, with buildings at a height of four stories. Arterials to the town center are lined with three- and four-story apartment clusters.

The Yanbu plan is a comprehensive one which addresses management problems and the unpredictable nature of future populations as well as physical form. The use of prototypes and modular units is an aid in communicating its essential urban design intentions to the many groups who will participate in its implementation.

Regional map.
1 Yanbu New Town
2 Yanbu
3 Red Sea
4 Airport
5 Yanbu-Jeddah highway
6 Industry

General view of Yanbu New Town towards the ▷ town center.

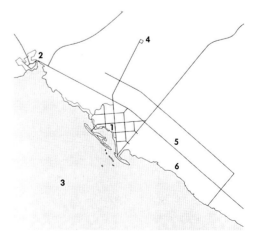

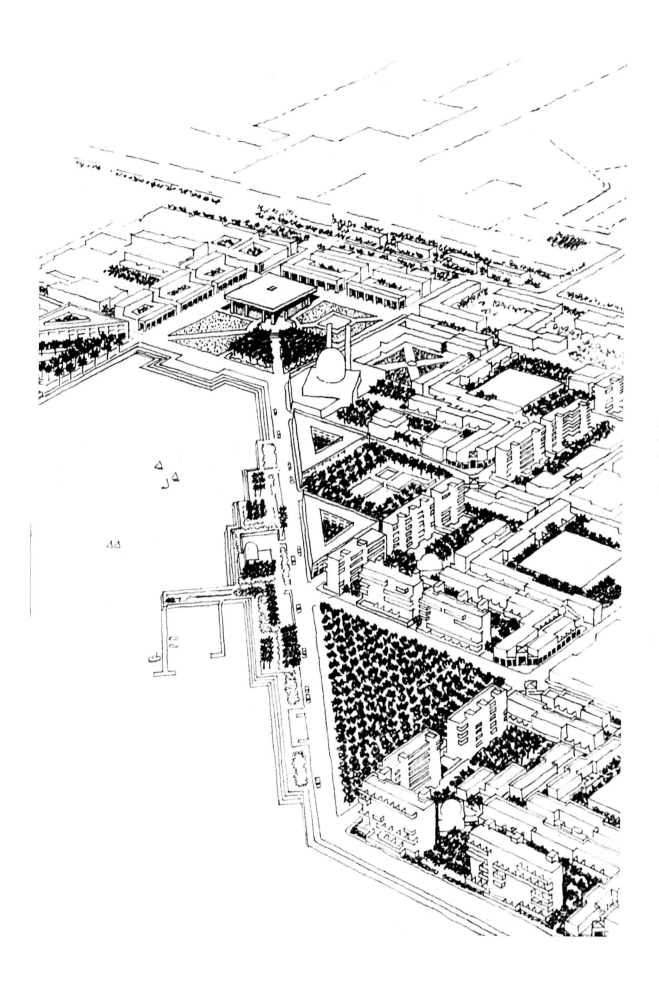

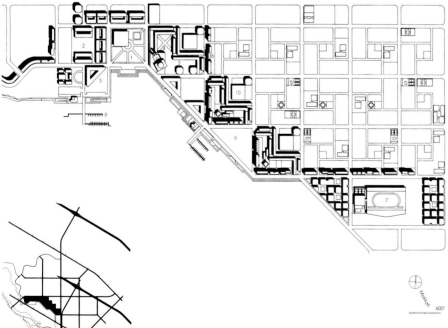

The focus of the town center is the civic plaza with the royal commission headquarters and the main mosque.

Plan of the town center.
1. Civic plaza and royal commission headquarters
2. Office
3. Souk
4. Mosque
5. Hotel
6. Elevator apartments
7. University and sports complex
8. Marinas
9. Commercial park
10. Parking
11. Coastal road and urban edge park

600'

Plan of a residential module.
 1 Elementary school
 2 Intermediate school
 3 Secondary school
 4 Mosque and commercial
 5 Arterial commercial
 6 Municipal services (clinic/social welfare)
 7 Cultural center
 8 Major open space
 9 Villas
10 Townhouses
11 Walk-up apartments

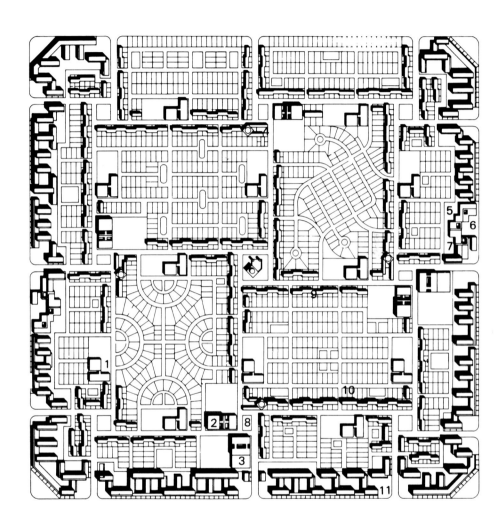

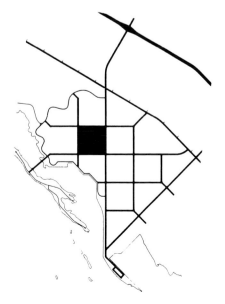

National Commercial Bank
Jeddah, Saudi Arabia

Traditionally, buildings in Saudi Arabia have spread out, but the irregular site and the desire to take advantage of spectacular views of the historic old city and the Red Sea led to the design of a high-rise structure. The 600,000-square-foot, 27-story triangular bank is flanked by a helical, 160,000-square-foot parking garage for 400 cars. Currently under construction on a 126,700-square-foot site between the old city and the sea, the project is scheduled for completion in 1983.

Instead of individual windows in the tower's outer travertine enclosure, colossal openings will allow views from, and light into, the interior across three landscaped courts that alternate position on two sides of the triangular shaft. Each of the resulting V-shaped floors of 18,000 square feet will thus be shielded from the direct effects of sun and wind, while a central wall that extends from the skylight of the first-floor banking hall through the roof will allow accumulated heat to rise out of the courts. In developing this form, SOM has incorporated at least two indigenous traditions: the principle of ventilation and – more importantly – the principle of turning the building inward. The office floors overlook the old city to the southeast through two seven-story openings and the Red Sea to the north through a nine-story opening.

Executives occupying the top floor where windows are recessed behind a sheltering arcade will have views in all directions. The chairman's suite, including the central boardroom, will occupy the entire south side of the building.

At ground level, the public banking hall will be a grand space. White and green marble floors repeat the pattern of the coffered concrete ceiling 30 feet above. A level for an auditorium, cafeteria, lounge and other common facilities will surround the lowest of the courts recessed into the steel tower. A core for elevators, stairs, toilets and other services has been placed at the third side of the triangular tower, allowing for flexible office space.

Plan (typical floor).

General view (model). ▷

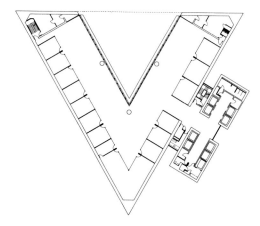

Plan (ground level).

Section. ▷

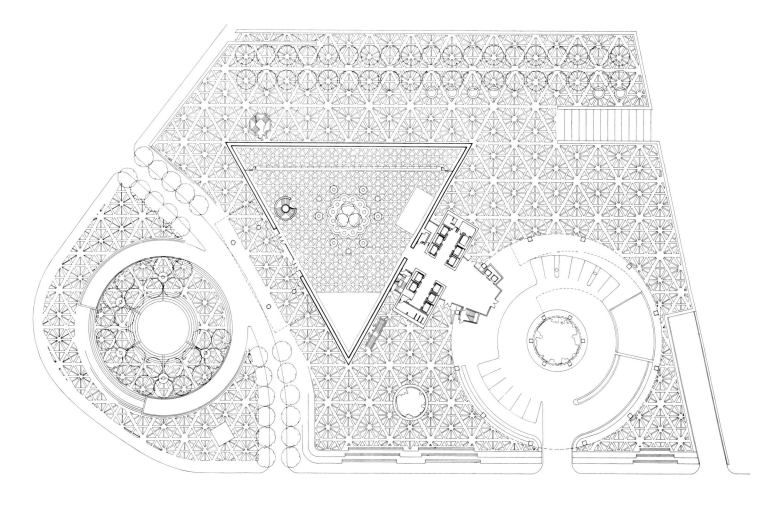

60'

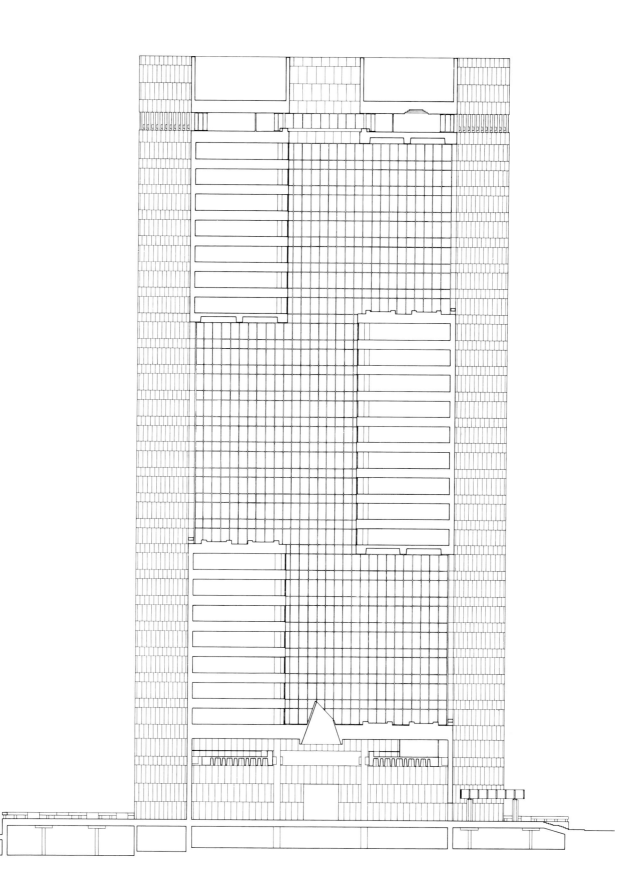

Haj Terminal, King Abdul Aziz International Airport
Jeddah, Saudi Arabia

The Haj Terminal at the King Abdul Aziz International Airport in Jeddah is located approximately 43.5 miles west of the Holy City of Makkah. Since Jeddah is the only large commercial city in close proximity to Makkah, all air traffic bound for Makkah arrives in Jeddah and proceeds by land transportation from Jeddah to Makkah. Normal airport facilities are capable of handling this traffic during most of the year; however, approximately once a year, vast numbers of Moslem pilgrims from all over the world travel to Makkah to participate in the Haj pilgrimage. The Haj activity takes place within about a six-week period, resulting in unusually high air traffic for this rather short period of time. Since the public facilities at the new airport were designed to handle only the normal flow of domestic and international air traffic, a separate terminal facility was required to process the Haj pilgrims.

The Haj Terminal design program required the facility to handle a large volume of people with highly diversified needs over a short period of time. It is projected that this facility will process approximately 950,000 pilgrims during the Haj by the year 1985. It is estimated that the terminal complex will need to accommodate 50,000 pilgrims at one time for periods up to 18 hours during arrival and 80,000 pilgrims for periods up to 36 hours during departure. This time is required in order to transfer between air and land transportation. Therefore, appropriate space, determined to be approximately 5,400,000 square feet, must be created which is adaptable and flexible to the Hajis' needs.

In response to these requirements, a scheme was developed which provided for a linear terminal building adjacent to the aircraft parking aprons and a large, sheltered support complex adjacent to the terminal building. This scheme provided for minimum walking distance for the pilgrims from the planes to the air-conditioned terminal where all formal processing and baggage handling are accomplished. The pilgrims then proceed into the naturally ventilated support area, where they will organize for travel by land to Makkah. Because of the rather severe environment in Jeddah, the support complex must be protected from the sun by a roof covering.

As it may take as many as 18 hours for the pilgrim to conclude the necessary preparations for the Haj, great care has been taken in the design of the support area to make the pilgrim's time in the area as pleasant as possible. Under each module, facilities are located for the pilgrim to rest, sleep and acquire both prepared foods or food which the pilgrim himself may prepare. In addition, many washing and toilet facilities have been provided in each module as well as offices providing banking, postal, airline, bus and taxi, and general information support services.

There are 210 semi-conical Teflon-coated Fiberglas roof units contained within a total of ten modules. Five modules located on each side of the central spine entry road cover a total area of approximately 105 acres. A single module contains 21 semi-conical fabric roof units stretched and formed by 32 radial cables. The modules are supported by 45-meter-high steel pylons located on a square 45 meter grid. The columns taper from 2.50 meters at their base to 1.00 meter at the top. In each module, steel cables radiate from the top of the columns to a 3.96-meter diameter central steel tension ring to which are attached the steel radial cables. The inherent long-span characteristics of steel cable structures allow for the spacing of columns to be far enough apart to give not only a very open feeling to the large support area but to allow for maximum flexibility in planning for the various support buildings located within the support area.

The form and height of the fabric roof units promote circulation of air from the open side of the support area up to and through the open steel tension ring located at the top of the roof unit. Mechanical fan towers placed intermittently between the columns enhance air circulation. Acoustical problems created by the many thousands of pilgrims located beneath the fabric roof are also diminished due to roof height and material. The fabric roofs provide shelter from intense desert heat. Because the fabric has a low heat transmission, it allows the sun to cast a warm light over the support area; at night, it will become a great reflective surface as pylon-mounted uplights bounce light from the roof to the ground below. Located under the landscaped central mall, two large exhaust fans for each module draw off exhaust fumes of the buses.

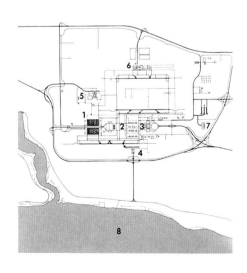

Location plan of the Haj Terminal.
1 Apron
2 Vehicle loading
3 Buses and taxis

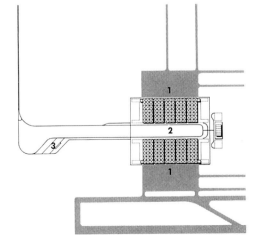

The tents, pylons, cables, and tension rings were designed as a single component and replicated to create the final complex. The tent design was described and drawn by the computer.

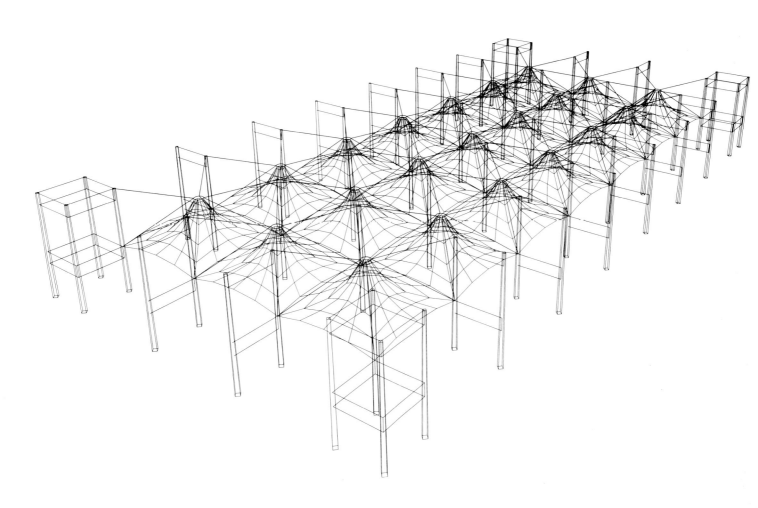

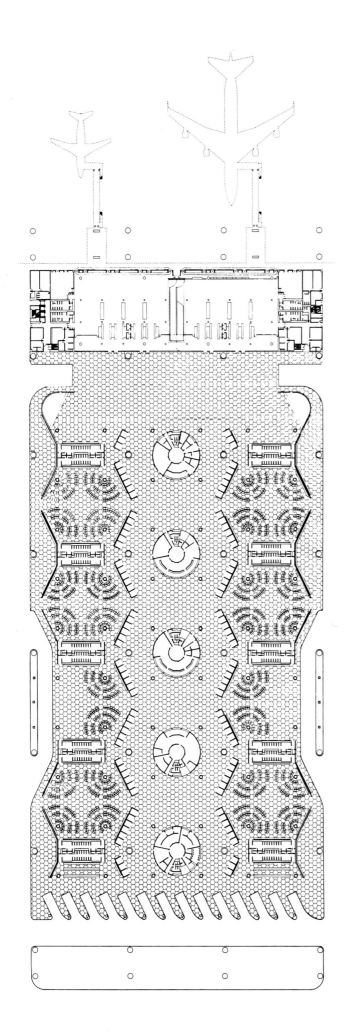

Plan of one of the ten modules.

Twenty wide-body aircraft gate positions – two ▷
at the short side of each module – are available.

Pages 284–285:
The Haj Terminal not only fulfills the requirements of its functional program, but also
provides a moving and uplifting experience to
the pilgrims as they set foot on the soil of the
holy land of Islam.

Photo Credits

Peter Aaron/ESTO 158 (14), 253, 255
Joe C. Aker 154–155 (1), 159 (18, 19), 164, 167
Jaime Ardiles-Arce 25, 66, 69, 70, 71, 191, 249, 250, 251
Guy Arnold 78 (5), 101
Morley Baer 20 (2, 4, 8)
Jeremiah O. Bragstad 21 (11), 22 (20), 157 (8)
Orlando R. Cabanban 13 (12), 15 (18), 78 (4), 81 (19, 21, 22), 82 (31), 157 (9, 10, 11), 235 (11), 236 (14)
Bill Engdahl/Hedrich-Blessing 79 (10), 100 bottom
Michael Fisher/ESTO 223 bottom
Bruce Forster 20 (5), 74, 75
Gorchev & Gorchev 209 right
Steve Grubman 79 (12), 106–107
Harlan Hambright 221
Harr/Hedrich-Blessing 82 (29), 97, 157 (12), 177 (23), 209 left
Hedrich-Blessing 12 (9), 76–77 (1), 78 (3, 6), 24, 125, 134, 136, 137
Jim Hedrich/Hedrich-Blessing 10 (2), 234 (5)
Bob Hollingsworth 13 (13), 14 (15), 14 (17), 17 (25), 21 (15), 22 (22), 23 (24, 25, 28, 29), 24, 27, 29, 31, 33, 35, 37, 43, 45, 53
Jack Horner 178 (25), 188, 200, 235 (12), 246
Thomas J. Houha/SOM 74, 236 (13)
Wolfgang Hoyt/ESTO 10 (3), 15 (19), 17 (24), 82 (28), 88, 89, 174 (2), 176 (13, 15, 16), 177 (19, 22), 178 (26, 27, 28, 29), 181, 183, 185, 187, 195, 196, 197, 201, 218, 219, 222, 223 top, 225, 227, 229, 235 (10)
Lawrence Hudetz 74
Timothy Hursley 42, 215
Greg Hursley/Hursley & Lark 16 (23), 158 (15)
Hursley/Lark/Hursley 161
Helmut Jacoby 176 (18)
Warren Jagger 176 (14)
Howard N. Kaplan/HNK Architectural Photography 11 (5), 14 (14), 16 (22), 98, 100 top, 237 (21)
Balthazar Korab 79 (8), 80 (17), 82 (27), 129, 131, 151, 153
Jay Langlais/Owens-Corning Fiberglas 237 (22), 281, 283, 284, 285, 286–287
Lewellyn Studio 78 (7)
Jane Lidz 23 (26, 27), 57, 58, 59
Erich Locker 172–173 (1)
Merrick/Hedrich-Blessing 14 (16), 16 (21), 78 (2), 80 (15), 81 (20), 82 (25), 85, 87, 120, 121, 127, 147
Joseph W. Moliter 175 (8)
Ronald Moore 10 (1), 22 (18)
Greg Murphy 82 (30)
Gerald Ratto 22 (21), 23 (23)
Steve Rosenthal 175 (10), 176 (11), 177 (20), 211, 213
Sadin/Karant Photography 143, 144–145
Paul Stevenson Oles, AIA 176 (17)
Stewart's, Inc. 13 (11), 156 (5)
Ezra Stoller/ESTO 11 (4), 11 (6), 12 (7, 8), 13 (10), 20 (7), 21 (13), 79 (9, 11), 80 (13, 14, 16), 82 (26), 105, 109, 111, 112–113, 116, 117, 118–119, 139, 141, 156 (2, 3, 4, 6, 7), 174 (3, 4), 175 (6, 7, 9), 193, 203, 205, 234 (7), 235 (9), 275
Sunderland Aerial Photography 21 (12)
Mak Takahashi 21 (9, 10, 14)
Wes Thompson 20 (6), 61, 63, 163
Union Carbide Corporation 174 (5)
Paul Warchol/ESTO 149
Wayne Thom Associates 15 (20), 18–19 (1), 22 (17, 19)
R. Wenkam 20 (3), 22 (16)
Nick Wheeler 81 (23), 177 (21), 206, 207, 235 (8), 239, 240, 241, 243, 244, 245